P9-DHA-860

A Ragged Mountain Press
WOMAN'S GUIDE

BACKPACKING

ADRIENNE HALL

Series Editor, Molly Mulhern Gross

Ragged Mountain Press
Camden, Maine

New York • San Francisco • Washington, D.C. • Auckland • Bogotá
Caracas • Lisbon • London • Madrid • Mexico City • Milan • Montreal
New Delhi • San Juan • Singapore • Sydney • Tokyo • Toronto

Look for these other Ragged Mountain Press Woman's Guides

Sea Kayaking, Shelley Johnson
Snowboarding, Julia Carlson
Mountaineering, Andrea Gabbard
Fly Fishing, Dana Rikimaru

Sailing, Doris Colgate
Canoeing, Laurie Gullion
Skiing, Maggie Loring
Snow Sports, Iseult Devlin

• •

International Marine/
Ragged Mountain Press ℞

A Division of The **McGraw·Hill** Companies

10 9 8 7 6 5 4 3 2

Library of Congress Cataloging-in-Publication Data
Hall, Adrienne
     A Ragged Mountain Press Woman's Guide: Backpacking / Adrienne Hall.
         p.   cm.
     Includes index.
     ISBN 0-07-026027-3 (pbk.)
     1. Backpacking. 2. Outdoor recreation for women.   I. Title.
GV199.6H35   1998
796.51—dc21   97-48591
                                                        CIP

Questions regarding the content of this book
should be addressed to:
Ragged Mountain Press
P.O. Box 220, Camden, ME 04843

Questions regarding the ordering of this book
should be addressed to:
The McGraw-Hill Companies
Customer Service Department
P.O. Box 547, Blacklick, OH 43004
Retail customers: 1-800-262-4729
Bookstores: 1-800-722-4726

Visit us on the World Wide Web at
www.raggedmountainpress.com

Printed by Quebecor Printing Company, Fairfield, PA
Edited by Cynthia Flanagan Goss; Kathryn Mallien
Design by Carol Inouye, Inkstone Communications Design
Project management by Janet Robbins
Page layout and production assistance by Shannon Thomas
Illustrations by Elayne Sears
Photo credits: Page 11, Cheyenne Rouse/Mountain Stock; Page
22, Cheyenne Rouse/Cheyenne Rouse Photography; Page 26,
Wendy Campbell/Ouside Images; Page 37, Peter Dennen/
Outside Images; Page 54, Ty Youngstrom/Outside Images;
Page 68, Larry Carver/Mountain Stock; Page 88, Cliff Leight;
Page 109, Cliff Leight; Page 115, Cliff Leight; Page 124, John
Laptad/ Uniphoto; Page 131, Ty Youngstrom/Outside Images;
Page 137, Daryl Hunter/Mountain Stock; Page 157, Cliff Leight
All other photos by the author unless otherwise indicated.

••

"I love mountaintops and lovely places
that you can get to only by hiking. I
will hike until I can no longer walk!"

—Mae Holt, age 60

••

Foreword

We were just catching our breath and quenching our hiker's thirst when two young women came up the trail behind and asked "Are you going across there?" This was the very question I was asking myself as I gazed across the Knife Edge, the infamous sliver of a trail separating Mt. Katahdin's Pamola Peak—where we stood—and Baxter Peak. On that August day the trail appeared and reappeared between sheets of fog blowing up and over its rocky, serrated edge.

Looking relieved when we answered yes, the pair had another question: "Mind if we tag along behind?"

"No, not at all," we replied in unison, and our expanded group struck out across the windblown rooftop of northern Maine. I didn't say a word during our 20-minute traverse of a trail no wider than the length of my arm, a trail from which the mountain falls away at an alarmingly steep angle on both sides. But once we reached the peak on the far side—where the trail widened to the broad expanse of flattened mountain top—I erupted into a mile-wide grin, and then laughter, nearly bursting with my accomplishment. It's that feeling that keeps me hiking and backpacking: setting a goal—be it the pristine lake two miles away or the summit thousands of feet above—and reaching it. But that trip also pushed me to the edge of my comfort zone, propelling me to a place I wasn't sure I wanted to be. As I hiked across that mountaintop trail I kept three points of my body touching the trail; when a particularly strong wind gust came along, I even got down on all fours.

Call me two-faced: Part of me wanted to go across, and part didn't. While I love trying new sports and activities, I often find myself at that edge, uncomfortable about what's expected of me, wondering if I'm really up to the challenge. Somehow on that day I put one foot in front of the other and tried not to look down. And once I'd made it, I was overjoyed.

I know now that I'd have been better off had I stopped to take a few deep breaths, assessed my inner voices (the ones yelling and screaming, telling me there was no way I'd possibly make it), and perhaps even uttered a bit about my fears to my companion. What I did gain from that experience was a need to find out if I was the only hiker in the world who had ever felt that way. I began looking for books and articles that addressed my concerns as an outdoorswoman. Pitching my tent alone always made me feel vulnerable: Was I making myself easy prey for unfriendly strangers? Were there ways to disguise the fact that I was alone, and was such a masquerade even necessary? (See Chapter 7 for great advice about personal safety in the woods.) As I hiked I often played out other scenes in my head: What would happen if I slipped on a summit and needed help?

Backpacking: A Woman's Guide answers those questions, providing instruction and advice I wish I'd had before heading across the Knife Edge. Here you'll find other women's backpacking experiences told in a manner that respects how women learn and grow.

What's so different about the way women learn? If you're like me, you want to hear a description of a move or tactic before launching into it. I'm a fan of the talk-it-over-and-think-it-through-first school of outdoor learning. I prefer to ask questions *before* I'm asked to traverse a slim pencil line of a trail, wobbling under the strain of a backpack. I want to hear advice from someone like me, someone I know and trust. And I like to learn in a group so I can hear other folks' questions—and know I'm not the only one wondering how to light the stove without singeing my eyebrows (see pages 84–85!).

We've done our best to mimic the learning conditions of a woman's instructional clinic in The Ragged Mountain Press Woman's Guides. Here you'll find lots of women's voices: your instructor's, of course, but also voices of women from all walks who love the outdoors. *Backpacking: A Woman's Guide* provides solutions, advice, and stories from women who have done what you are about to do: learn to backpack. I hope Adrienne's words and approach help get you out exploring and enjoying, by yourself or with a friend. I'll look for you out there.

Between backpacking trips, drop us a note to tell us how we're doing and how we can improve these guides to best suit you and your learning style.

MOLLY MULHERN GROSS
Series Editor, The Ragged Mountain Press Woman's Guides
Camden, Maine
April 1998

An avid outdoorswoman, Molly Mulhern Gross enjoys running, hiking, camping, sea kayaking, telemark skiing, in-line skating, and biking and has just started snowboarding. She is Director of Editing, Design, and Production at Ragged Mountain Press and International Marine.

Contents

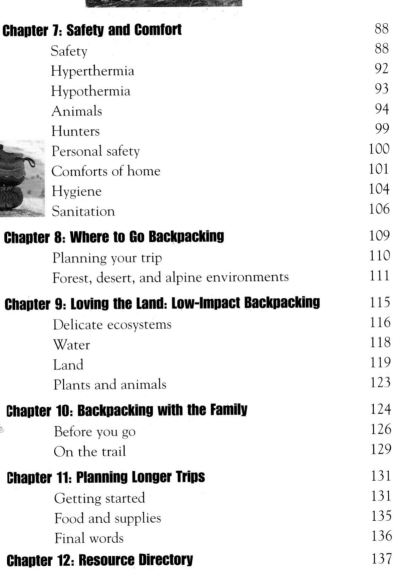

CONTENTS

Acknowledgments

I'd like to offer a sincere thank you to all the women backpackers who responded so candidly to my survey. Your comments, stories, and advice are sure to make the path a little easier for women who are just getting started. I'd also like to acknowledge the many friends, family members, and new acquaintances who demonstrated techniques, modeled gear, and shared memorable backpacking moments in photographs throughout the book.

A sincere thank you to my family, who encouraged me to pursue my dreams and promised to stand by me, even when I decided to walk for six months instead of going to graduate school!

Thanks to Molly Mulhern Gross, series editor, for taking the initiative to develop her idea into reality. I also want to thank Molly Mulhern Gross and Jeff Serena for their continued support and enthusiasm, and Kate Mallien and Cynthia Flanagan Goss who worked hard to sculpt and polish the manuscript.

O n July 28, 1996, I completed a six-month trek of the Appalachian Trail. My journal entry for that day reads,

> The moment I had been waiting six months for arrived today. The mountain that was my dream became a dot on the horizon, then a distant peak. This morning the base of Mt. Katahdin, the northern terminus of the Appalachian Trail, was beneath my feet. As I began the 4,000-foot climb, my thoughts reeled back to February 15—the day I saw the first blaze of the Appalachian Trail on Springer Mountain in Georgia. I was so fresh, so naive, so anxious to begin the trek to Maine. I remembered how sore my feet were after the first day, the blisters that plagued my feet for six weeks, and the foot pains that never did go away. I remembered the inspiring views, the good-spirited hikers, the fresh air.
>
> Six months is a long time to be in the woods: There's a lot of time for self-doubt. With only 5 miles left on a 2,159-mile hike, I finally thought that I might finish. The sign atop Katahdin that marks the end of the trail was branded in my mind. I had seen it photographed a hundred times. . . . The wooden sign was now 20 yards away. I moved towards it and reached out to touch it. Tears welled up in my eyes as I read the bottom line on the sign. Next to an arrow pointing south, it read, "Springer Mountain, Georgia—2,135 miles."

My trek of the Appalachian Trail was the climax of my backpacking adventures, and I love reading my journals and reliving those moments. I wish I had kept journals of my earliest attempts at backpacking and camping. Still, I can recall the first time I camped in the woods.

I was nine and my brother, Scott, was six. My parents packed us in the back of our tan Oldsmobile and headed west from Philadelphia to one of Pennsylvania's state parks. We drove to a level spot and set up camp. I remember our green canvas tent, shaped like a house. I helped fit together the heavy metal rods that framed the tent. We unloaded lawn chairs, blankets, coolers filled with fruit, sandwiches, and juice boxes. My brother and I entertained ourselves for hours— throwing rocks into the creek, overturning logs and collecting roly-poly bugs, and running through the woods. I remember the smell of grease in the morning as I squatted over the "buddy burner" stove I'd made in Brownies. I lit a fire under the inverted tin can and fried bacon on the top, and then I fried an egg in the bacon grease for my brother.

The summer before I started seventh grade, my mom once again coerced Scott and me into our Oldsmobile. This time we headed out for thirty-three days of camping across the United States. We divided the back seat with an imaginary line, mom gave us Road Trip Bingo, and off we went.

I still remember many details of that trip: the sound of bats' leathery wings flapping at the mouth of the Carlsbad Caverns in New Mexico; the dry heat of the Grand Canyon; circular hay bales in Texas fields; the stench of rotten eggs from the sulfur pits at Yellowstone. That trip made such a strong impression on me because we hiked the land, slept in it, drank it.

It wasn't until college that I began to go on real backpacking trips. I left the lawn chairs and hibachi behind and headed into the woods for days at a time. The Blue Ridge Mountains were less than a two-hour drive from my school in Virginia. I began to realize that backpacking is an enjoyable form of exercise. It was a different experience every time—a new trail, new terrain, a different hiking partner, different weather conditions. Backpacking was also the best way I knew to release the stresses of school.

During my college years, I spent summers in the Rocky Mountains of Colorado, where I worked at an outdoor outfitting store. Although I never made a good salesperson (I felt uncomfortable trying to get people to buy things), I learned how to properly layer clothes and how to fit boots, and I picked up other backpacking tips.

During that time I also experimented with food. I remember descending from a rocky summit and arriving at a campsite exhausted and famished. I removed a can of soup from my pack, and then it hit me: I didn't have a can opener. I pounded holes in the top of the can with a tent stake and a rock. Soon afterward I learned about lighter foods that required fewer utensils.

After college, I moved out West and continued exploring and hiking and learning. I *had* to see what was over the next pass. I learned by going out there and getting wet, then going out again and staying dry. I learned by carrying too much weight, then getting rid of the deodorant, the baseball hat, and the can of soda for a more comfortable load. I became confident about my ability to survive without civilization.

When I prepared for my 2,159-mile hike of the Appalachian Trail, I read book after book about what to expect, how many miles to walk per day, and how to prepare food drops. But I was doubtful that the information in those books applied to me, for none of the books I read were written by women. I wanted a woman's voice to tell me that she had completed a long-distance hike, and that I could too. I wanted *her* opinions and advice. I wanted to know how much weight she carried and if she felt comfortable sleeping in crowded shelters. I needed someone to tell me what to do when I got my period. But that someone wasn't there for me. I had to figure things out the hard way, but I hope I can be that someone for you.

There is a gap in current outdoor recreation literature. We need more books for women, written by women. Even today, when I tell men that I am writing a book on backpacking for women, they often look puzzled and reply, "Why? Is it different for women?" Yes, it is different. Women are physically different from men. We have different needs, different concerns, and oftentimes different goals and experiences. Women can learn more about backpacking if we are taught by other women.

In this book I share what I and dozens of other women have learned from our experiences in the wilderness. In preparing this book, I sent questionnaires to every corner of the United States and queried female backpackers who have spent years mastering their techniques. They offered advice and shared their successes and failures.

Chapter 1

THE FEMALE BACKPACKER

WHAT IS BACKPACKING?

First, let's define what we mean by backpacking. How is it different from hiking and camping?

Hiking and camping are the two components of backpacking. If you walk for a day in the woods, you can say you went hiking. If you bike or canoe to a campsite and sleep outdoors, you can say you went camping. But only if you carry all your supplies into the wilderness and spend the night can you say that you went backpacking.

Backpacking requires you to be totally self sufficient. You don't have a car to transport your belongings or a house to come back to at night. Whether you spend one night or a hundred nights hiking and sleeping outside, you can consider yourself a backpacker.

WHAT IT TAKES

Backpacking is an activity almost anyone can do. Walking is the most basic form of transportation and the only one that allows you to move slowly enough to truly see the natural environment around you. It is difficult to smell sagebrush and ponderosa pines, or hear woodpeckers and owls, when you're traveling 50 mph in a metal box on wheels.

My favorite aspect of backpacking is knowing I can go to a place only accessible by foot.

A backpacker navigates rocky terrain. (Bob Allen/Outside Images)

Many hiking trails are not accessible to mountain bikes or off-road vehicles. The rewards of finding a spectacular spot—a scenic overlook, a secluded lake—are far greater when you have to work to get there. Think of all the people who will never travel beyond pavement. They will never see these hidden treasures. But you will.

Backpacking is about physical exertion, personal challenge, exploration, oneness with nature, and personal fulfillment. Some women feel they are too old for the sport, but you are *never* too old to backpack. Sixty-year-old Mae Holt is a woman who knows that backpacking has no age limit. "I love mountaintops and lovely places that you can get to only by hiking," she says. "I will hike until I can no longer walk!"

You don't have to be athletic or naturally coordinated to backpack—you just need a positive attitude. When you're climbing a mountain and your thigh muscles are burning, tell yourself you can do it—because you can. (You'll find great information on getting fit for backpacking in Chapter 3, page 26.)

On the Appalachian Trail I met women in their sixties and seventies who had been trekking through the mountains for weeks. Other older women were maintaining the trail, sawing felled trees, and clearing branches from the trail.

Rose Magnarella, 67, and Virginia Talbot, 60, maintain sections of the Appalachian Trail in North Carolina. They advise beginners to go with an experienced person who can check your equipment or take a course with a hiking organization like Elderhostel (listed in the Resource Directory, page 142).

Rather than worry about leaving your children, take them along. What better way to instill in children a respect for the environment than to take them out there and let them explore it

"Experiencing nature on any backpacking trip compensates for all the sore muscles and blistered feet. There is just nothing like it!"

—Jane Gallagher Kaopuiki, age 83

themselves? The February 1996 issue of *Backpacker* magazine featured a family with eight children, the youngest age two and the oldest age fifteen. This family had graduated from car camping to extensive backpacking trips. At the time the article was written, they were planning a seven-month hike of the Continental Divide Trail. Of course, not everyone wants to camp with their children for seven months! (You'll find more on backpacking with children on page 124.)

Backpacking is one sport where speed is discouraged. It's not a race. Take your time. Notice what's around you. Bring a wildflower guide or a bird book and try to identify what you see. When you get tired, stop for a scenery break. Take pictures. Keep a journal.

To spend one night or one week in the wilderness requires a willingness to live without the amenities of civilization. You'll soon realize how good it feels to be self sufficient and to carry on your back everything you need. As backpacker Catherine Shade says, "If you are willing to forgo modern conveniences for a little while and are able to endure a few aches and pains, the rewards are worth it all." The more things you leave behind, the lighter your pack will be, making your walk more comfortable and enjoyable. (Chapter 5 includes details on efficient packing; see page 54.)

You will also need to adapt to changing conditions. If it starts to rain or if the campsite isn't what you expected, try to make the best of it. Nature is unpredictable. The best you can do is play with the cards you've been dealt. And remember that trips made in less than favorable conditions make the best stories!

Backpacking requires that you work to get where you want to go and that you get a little dirty in the process. You can live with a little dirt and sweat for a few days. When you get home, I guarantee you that a shower will never have felt so good.

To be a backpacker you need to be willing to live in nature, to get in synch with the natural cycles of light and darkness, to respect the environment and capitalize on what it has to offer, to let your curiosity and spirit of adventure keep you going, and to relax and have fun.

• •

"The hike that day was one of my most memorable experiences. Every component was present: companionship, laughs, sun, amazing blue sky. We explored five lakes at the base of the Continental Divide and hiked down their grassy, glowing ridges at sunset. Coming down, all I could say was that I couldn't possibly imagine being anywhere else."

—Stacy Middleton, age 26

• •

"I prefer one-night trips. I have two children—ages three and six—and they (and I) cannot muster the energy for anything more. But when they get older, I'll hike the Long Trail with them and do bigger trips."

—Jennifer Botzojorn, age 33

• •

"If you are willing to forgo modern conveniences for a little while and are able to endure a few aches and pains, the rewards are worth it all. For no other way can you experience nature in all its aspects."

—Catherine Shade, age 69

WHO BACKPACKS?

The first female mountaineers trekked the Alps in their traditional attire of skirts and dresses in the early 1800s. One of the first American women mountain climbers was Julia Archibald Holmes. In 1858, at age 20, she became the first woman of record to climb the 14,110-foot Pikes Peak in the Colorado Rockies. And she broke the female dress code by wearing bloomers instead of a dress.

By the 1920s, the idea of women climbing mountains had become slightly more acceptable. Hiking clubs—such as the Appalachian Mountain Club (formed in 1876), the Sierra Club (1892), and the Colorado Mountain Club (1912)—were established. Both women and men were welcome to join.

By 1940, over three dozen women had pursued the fledgling sport of mountain climbing in the Colorado Rockies. Many women did it because they wanted to see what was "up there." Some were botanists who collected plants on the mountains. Two women, Virginia McClurg and Lucy Peabody, climbed mountains to visit and preserve Native American ruins; they were ultimately responsible for establishing a national park to preserve the cliff dwellings at Mesa Verde.

One of backpacking's most famous pioneers was a woman named Emma "Grandma" Gatewood. In 1955, at the age of 67, she became the first woman and the eighth person to survive a continuous hike the length of the Appalachian Trail. A corn and tobacco farmer and grandmother to twenty-three children, she was a workaholic and was unable to leave her Ohio home until she was in her sixties. When she set out to hike the then-1,200-mile AT by herself, she didn't tell a single person. She wore Keds high-top sneakers and carried a duffel bag.

By 1969 Grandma Gatewood had hiked 10,000 miles—more than any other woman. (Photo courtesy of Appalachian Trail Conference)

A few years later, Grandma Gatewood became the first person to through-hike the Appalachian Trail (hike continuously from end to end) three times. In 1959, at the age of 71, she hiked the 2,000-mile Oregon Trail from Independence, Missouri, to Portland, Oregon. And by 1969 she had hiked 10,000 miles—more miles than any other woman. "I want to see what's on the other side of the hill," she said, "then what's beyond that. The forest is a quiet place and nature is beautiful. I don't want to sit and rock. I want to do something." (Excerpted from *Walking the Appalachian Trail* by Larry Luxenberg, Stackpole Books, 1994.)

"Forget about how your hair looks. Leave anything in a glass bottle at home. Leave anything cotton at home. Take a warmer sleeping bag than you think you need and take a set of dry clothes."

—Elizabeth Fox, age 55

The Appalachian Trail Conference estimates that the percentage of women attempting a continuous hike of the AT increased from around 10 percent in the late 1980s and early 1990s to an estimated 20 to 22 percent in 1997. Other sources suggest that one-third of all hikers are women.

Women of all ages and abilities are on the trails. Many of them grew up backpacking with their families and friends. As Sara Hurley, age 24, recalls, "My parents took us camping—out of cars, canoes, bikes—ever since I can remember. I took a hiatus from it all during high school and in the beginning of college. While on a semester abroad in East Africa, I backpacked for two two-week segments and fell in love with it for myself. I've lived in the backcountry for the better part of the two years since I graduated."

Many women developed a love for backpacking after they joined a hiking club in the community, in school, or in college. Anne Thiessen, age 36, credits the Girl Scouts with fostering her interest: "I was in a troop full of great girls and very active parents. This troop became a hiking club with snow trips, cross country desert trips, trips with the local mountain rescue squad and university groups. Backpacking became one of the best parts of my life and helped me find a positive identity during the teen years."

"I have walked all my life because my family never owned a vehicle. I got started hiking in 1983 when my husband and I discovered two books: *Hiking the Appalachian Trail*, Volumes 1 and 2."

—Mae Holt, age 60

Other women got involved later in life. Many of these women are mothers, women in the work force, and retired women. Rose Magnarella, age 67, explains, "I love the woods—hiking and being outdoors. Two friends and I were Girl Scout leaders. When we discovered the Appalachian Trail passed one corner of the Girl Scout camp, we

• •

"**A** friend of the family was hiking the Appalachian Trail. When he stopped to visit he convinced me to take my vacation time and hike with him as far as I could. My first backpack trip was 300 miles. [I had] no experience at all. The trip was the best experience I ever had until I hiked the entire trail from Georgia to Maine myself."

—Kathy Kelly Borowski, age 37

• •

decided to backpack from Pawling, New York, to Kent, Connecticut. We did it on weekends and overnight trips."

Women are increasing their numbers on trails all over the world, from Norway to Italy, from Canada to Australia. These women share a common interest: They want to explore a beautiful place, challenge themselves, and grow. And although our equipment has changed (we no longer carry duffel bags or wear cotton dresses), the same determination that got Julia Archibald Holmes and Grandma Gatewood up mountain after mountain carries us a long way.

WHY BACKPACK?

We backpack for a number of reasons: the pleasure of seeing a beautiful place, the feeling of independence that increases with each trip, the confidence it helps us gain in other aspects of our lives. Many women embrace the challenge and adventure of backpacking and thrive on the opportunity for personal achievement. Few things compare to the feeling of completing a challenging hike.

From Canada to Australia, women are showing up on the trails in greater numbers. (Photo of Bugaboos, Canada, by Brooks Dodge/Mountain Stock)

• •

"It was the third pass of the day and I was already pushing myself, hiking with a 50-pound pack at 11,000 feet. Self-doubt crept into my brain: What if I can't make it up that pass? What then? The three strong men I was with weren't struggling at all. At the base of the third pass I peered up the talus slope and had to hold back tears. I had no choice. I kept moving my feet and I counted my breaths, matching an inhale with each step, pausing after ten. I entered a meditative state and my mental self took over. I had never experienced that before. Before I knew it, I was at the top taking in a breathtaking 360-degree view. I had just pushed my physical and mental limits further than I had ever thought possible, and at that moment I realized I can do anything. Mental and physical strength are intimately intertwined. You have to hone both to live a lifestyle dedicated to adventure."

—Amy McMullen, age 25

• •

When you give everything you've got and forget why you are even climbing the mountain, often that's when you're rewarded with a view more spectacular than you ever imagined.

Reflecting the current revival of earth-based spirituality, some women spend time in wildlands to commune with nature, connect with the energy of the earth, and meditate. There is an extreme peace found in nature. The longer you spend immersed in it, the more connected you will feel. For hiker Stacy Middleton, there's no better way to communicate with the earth: "Because of the connection I make with nature, nothing contents me the way backpacking does. Backpacking is a good way to get in touch with Mother Earth, and women and the earth have a lot in common. I hold the deepest respect for [Mother Earth]. The closer I can get to Her, the better I feel."

People often take to the woods for its healing qualities. Many hikers seek solace in wildlands

• •

"I got started by camping with a group of friends in Yellowstone. I was equipped with a tiny school backpack with ropes holding everything in place. I had to borrow everyone's equipment. Having grown up in the plains of North Dakota, I honestly did not know backpacking existed. But after a summer in Yellowstone I was hooked. It has been a passion of mine ever since."

—Stacy Middleton, age 26

• •

. . . .

"Backpacking should not just be viewed as a popular sport that's good for your body. For some of us, the trails have led to a better understanding of our relationship with the land and all of its inhabitants."

—Jody Bickel, age 25

. . . .

after a divorce, death of a loved one, job loss, or bad test score—or they simply go to evaluate their life and sort out who they are and what they want to do. One woman found in nature an aid to her recovery process: "I sat in AA meetings for ten years, learning and learning. . . . I relive all that I have learned every time I take a swim in a swift river, provide that much-needed Ziploc to a fellow backpacker, or look out over a breathtaking view and know that I am not alone."

Other women crave the connection with nature that backpacking provides. My interest in biology and natural history inspired me to muddy my boots and take a closer look at the natural world. When I backpack, I often identify wildflowers and observe animals. I have also discovered trends in nature that are useful for backpacking: I've noticed that cottonwoods and willows usually grow near a water source; that birds make a distinct call when an animal or another person is approaching; that animals are very active before a storm, then remain calm right before it hits. I've become familiar with the contours of the land and can predict where a trail will go. Backpacking is an excellent way to explore the land around you and study its natural history.

Many women enjoy backpacking for its tremendous health benefits. Backpacking will make you burn more calories, improve your heart, and strengthen your muscles and bones. Your basal metabolic rate (BMR) is the number of calories you burn doing nothing. Your metabolism increases when your body has more muscle to feed. Since walking with a loaded backpack builds

. . . .

"I am a recovering addict, thirteen years. Addiction took away everything—my self-esteem, my ability to feel. . . . Without those things, I lived in fear most of my life. I sat in AA meetings for ten years, learning and learning. When I finally had the courage to put what I learned to the test, nature was there to continue my journey. I never thought that by learning through nature I would be able to feel so damn good. I relive all that I have learned every time I take a swim in a swift river, provide that much-needed Ziploc to a fellow backpacker, or look out over a breathtaking view and know that I am not alone."

—an intermediate backpacker, age 33

. . . .

Backpackers find beauty and companionship in Southern California's Joshua Tree National Park. (Photo by Cheyenne Rouse Photography)

muscle, backpacking elevates your BMR. Even when you're resting, your body burns more calories if you're in good shape.

Hiking with a loaded backpack for only 30 to 45 minutes twice a week will improve your cardiovascular fitness. Additionally, because basic backpacking does not include a flight stage (an instant when both your feet are off the ground at the same time), it puts little stress on your joints and causes fewer injuries than running or jogging does.

The thickness and strength of your bones depend, in large part, on how and how much you exercise. For this reason, a weight-bearing activity such as backpacking is useful in preventing and reversing an age-related weakening of the bones, or osteoporosis. Women typically add to their bone mass until they're in their early thirties.

"I had always been involved in athletics, from grammar school through college. My parents would take me camping every summer when I was growing up, and I found 'roughing it' to be right up my alley. When organized sports were through for me, I needed something that could keep me in shape and allow me to be outdoors. There is a certain peace in backpacking that no sport could ever match."

—Cindy Shinderman, age 25

Backpacking's benefits are innumerable. (Photo by John Laptad, Uniphoto)

After that time, we lose bone for the rest of our lives. Backpacking increases the uptake of calcium if you are in the bone-gaining stage of your life, and it will decrease the rate at which you lose bone if you are in the bone-losing stage. This is very important, since 40 to 50 percent of women over age 45 develop bone problems due to osteoporosis.

There is no question that backpacking is a good workout. Besides, the beauty of a wildflower meadow and the serenade of chirping birds are far more inspiring than a sterile weight room and the grinding of Stairmasters. In the words of avid backpacker Cindy Shinderman, "There is a certain peace in backpacking that no sport could ever match."

Every year, thousands of people spend a portion of their free time hiking and camping. And although our motivations may differ, there's one reason for backpacking that we all share: It's fun!

Chapter 2

HOW TO BE A GOOD BEGINNER

GETTING STARTED

The best advice I can give a beginning backpacker is to start small and go with someone who is experienced. To get an idea of what backpacking is like, spend two nights in the woods and walk less than ten miles a day.

I prefer to start out small on any backpacking trip. Even if you feel you can go farther, stop after five miles. The last thing you want to do is develop blisters or overwork your muscles on the first day. Veteran backpacker Liz Alcack offers advice to first-time backpackers, "Go slow uphill, use good posture, and don't go too far the first day. Take care of your feet; take care of hot spots before they become blisters. Drink before you get thirsty and eat before you get hungry."

If you don't know anyone who backpacks, ask a local hiking club or outdoor outfitter. They often lead groups or can give you information about nearby hiking clubs. If you start asking around, a friendly, experienced backpacker will surely pop up. For more on networking and backpacking resources, see the Resource Directory, page 137.

Before you go, consult with a friend or partner about equipment; a veteran will know what you need. See if you can borrow some from a friend or rent what you need from an outfitter.

"**W**hen things seem tough, stop. Take a look around you and appreciate where you are and the courage it took to get there. Be deliberate about everything you do: How you place your feet, how you pack your pack, where you camp. Careful backpackers reap rewards."

—Kayden, age 26

Remember that comfort will be the key to enjoying yourself, so be sure anything you use fits you well. For details about equipment, see Chapter 4.

When you are on a trip, ask questions. Have your partner show you how to erect the tent, light the stove, use the water filter, read the compass. Then do it yourself. This truly is the best way to learn. I watched my boyfriend use a stove during a couple trips, and I thought I had the idea. But when I bought my own stove, I took it out of the package, put it on the ground, and had no idea what to do with it! Oftentimes, observing isn't enough.

Once you feel confident using your equipment and traveling through the wilderness, set out on a longer trip. A four- or five-day excursion will give you enough time to absorb your surroundings and get into a routine. Build on your successes.

Hiking clubs, outdoor organizations, and magazines offer lots of ideas about backpacking destinations. Many of these are listed in the Resource Directory, page 137. You'll also find specific destination information and learn how to find information about destinations in Chapter 8, page 109.

After you have a successful weekend trip, hike a more strenuous or more remote trail. Experiment with food and spice up your meals. Choose a trail you have always wanted to hike and lead the way—instead of following someone else's boot prints. Soon, *you* will be the one showing others how to do it.

MENTAL PREPARATION

One way to prepare for a backpacking trip is to visualize yourself on the trail. Even if you don't know exactly what to expect, visualize what you think it will be like.

I used to play soccer and lacrosse. Every night before a competition, my coaches urged us to visualize ourselves scoring a goal or making a perfect pass. Many professional athletes use this technique. It makes sense: If you've already accomplished a goal in your mind, it won't be as difficult when you are trying to physically accomplish it.

Picture yourself hiking uphill, being challenged, and making it to the top. See yourself gazing out over a spectacular view. Feel the sun on your cheeks, a breeze against your skin, damp hair sticking to your forehead. Picture a night of cool breezes, bright stars, and sound sleep. Imagine enjoying food and appreciating clean water more than you ever have. Visualize encountering bad weather and deciding what to do about it. Walk through your trip in your mind the night before you leave—you will find it easier to walk the next day.

Dori McDonald packs her backpack along the Brooks Range, Alaska. (Photo by Tom Bol/Outside Images)

BE A LOW-MAINTENANCE WOMAN

Deciding what to bring on a trip can be one of the most difficult parts of backpacking. We often feel as if we need to bring many things. But if we bring them all, we will surely collapse under the weight!

Deciding what to leave at home is a tough decision, because there are many things that you absolutely *do* need to survive. I will talk about those kinds of items in Chapter 5 (page 55), but here I want to discuss the things you might believe are vital to your existence but in reality are unnecessary. These things will only weigh you down.

• •

"There is a great deal you can learn from books and talking to others. Be prepared. Study your mountain guide before you go and know your route. Be aware of water: Will you have to cross any and will it be available for drinking? Have a first-aid kit and know how to use it. Be forever aware of the weather: Know the forecast and always carry gear for any condition. Most importantly, know your limitations and set only realistic goals for yourself."

—Laurie MacKenzie Gordon, age 37

• •

Left: Alison Kiesel cooling off in Canyonlands, Utah (photo by David Wheelock/Uniphoto). Center: Pacific Crest Trail (photo by Eric Sanford/ Mountain Stock). Right: Utah desert hiking (photo by Leighton White/ Mountain Stock).

The trick is to be a low-maintenance woman. The first step is to leave all makeup at home. The trees don't care how you look. Seasoned backpackers who practice a lightweight, low-maintenance lifestyle consider the idea of occupying space in their pack with makeup instead of food an extremely foolish idea.

Under no circumstance should you bring perfume, lotion (except sunblock), or deodorant. Trust me: Deodorant doesn't help anyway. No jewelry, no hair products, no brushes. Bring a small comb for longer trips. If you have long hair, you may want to pack hairbands or clips to keep it out of your face and off your neck.

You can also cut weight by scaling things down. Bring a tiny flashlight or headlamp, as

"**S**tart out with a short trip in good weather to ensure a positive experience and build on that. Read up to be fully prepared. Stick with it. If it gets hard, continue taking ten steps at a time. Walk slower rather than taking too many breaks. Solve problems while walking; dream; enjoy the scenery. Be proud of yourself for getting off your butt. Spread around your pleasure to get more women interested."

—Gael Lord, age 54

• •

"Take a long, luxurious shower before leaving; then plan on getting dirty! Plan on wearing the same shirt and shorts every day, and if you're feeling decadent, sneak in a change of underwear. You don't need makeup or even soap; a little gravel from the bottom of a stream beats Apri Apricot Facial Scrub any day. This is your chance to get dirty, be dirty, and enjoy it. Don't bring a ton of clothes and your entire medicine cabinet! Bring the essential basics and remember that everything you bring, you are carrying on *your* back."

—Brooke Zanatell, age 25

• •

opposed to a large one. Bring a small amount of toothpaste, not the whole tube. If you insist on bringing toilet paper, save partially used rolls before the trip so you don't have to pack a bulky roll. You don't need individual serving bowls and lots of utensils; eat out of the pot and carry only a spoon. You also don't need Kleenex or a big towel; a bandanna will do.

No cellular phones, portable disc players, or portable televisions should come with you. These items have no place in the woods. You are going backpacking to get away from all the things that clutter your life. The more baggage from the modern world you lug around with you, the more it will prevent you from enjoying a true wilderness experience.

You will soon discover that you can live comfortably with minimal supplies. And if you need something you don't have with you, you learn to improvise. A couple years ago I took my mom backpacking, and she wanted to bring a pillow. I eventually convinced her to put clothes in her sleeping bag's stuff sack at night. Soft clothes, such as fleece jackets, make comfortable pillows.

When I prepare for a hike, I usually pack, unload, throw out a few things, pack again, throw out a few more things, and still pack too much. Cindy Shinderman, veteran Appalachian Trail through-hiker, says, "My rule is: If I don't use an item *every* day, I probably don't need it at all." This is excellent advice about an important first step for the beginner backpacker.

Chapter 3

FIT FOR BACKPACKING

BUILDING FITNESS

If you think you are not strong enough to walk many miles with a fully loaded backpack, you're not alone. When I asked experienced female backpackers what aspect of backpacking they feared as a beginner, most worried they would not be strong enough to do it. "I was afraid I wouldn't be able to carry everything I thought I needed," said 29-year-old Cally Leach. For Amy McMullen, 25, "Most of my beginning backpacking was done with men—my father, brothers, boyfriends. I was worried I wouldn't be strong enough to keep up."

Many women overcome this fear by plunging in and doing it. "I kept hiking. I kept experiencing myself as a backpacker. I overcame my mind's opinion of my strength and found that I am stronger than I imagined," said Cally Leach.

Experienced backpacker and world traveler Brooke Zanatell offers an interesting perspective. "It is a wonderful and joyous thing to be a woman, and we must embrace those things that make us different from men. But we should not dwell on those differences until they become impediments to our own growth and adventuresome spirits," she advises. "Any woman who is questioning whether or not she is strong enough to be a backpacker should remember that backpacking is a *recreational sport* in America and Europe, but in many third world countries it is a matter of *survival*. Women between the ages of ten and eighty must walk far distances to collect firewood. They carry the wood in bundles on their backs without the help of internal frame backpacks, Gore-Tex, or hiking boots."

Surely, if they can do it, you can too.

Your body is the most important piece of equipment you will use for backpacking. It needs to perform all day and transport a lot of weight that it is not accustomed to supporting. It is important to care for your body so it functions as well as possible when you're on a trip.

In backpacking, there are trails to suit

• •

"It is a wonderful and joyous thing to be a woman, and we must embrace those things that make us different from men. But we should not dwell on those differences until they become impediments to our own growth and adventuresome spirits."

—Brooke Zanetell

• •

every level of ability. Beyond a basic level of fitness, some trails require no special physical preparation. You don't need to be a trained athlete to have a successful and exciting backpacking trip! However, some training may be necessary to prepare your body for fast hiking, high-altitude hiking, or long-distance trips. As in any physical activity, the better prepared you are, the more comfortable you'll be during a hike. Consider your present fitness level and the type of trail you'll be hiking; then dedicate as much time and effort to training as you think you'll need to achieve your trip goals. Generally, if you're at an average fitness level, you'll need to spend thirty minutes each day stretching and strengthening your backpacking muscles to prime your body for your next outing.

• •

"Women have amazing stamina and strength, especially when we can go at our own pace and not try to keep up with the guys. Many women are more apt to relax and enjoy the scenery without being so goal oriented."

—Anne Thiessen, age 36

• •

Exercise program

There are six large muscle groups that you should strengthen before you go backpacking: abdominals, calves, gluteus, quadriceps, hamstrings, and your back.

Before you work your muscles, it is important to warm up properly and stretch out. Warm up for at least five minutes. Gradually increase your heart rate and loosen your muscles. Jog, bike, do aerobics, jumping jacks—whatever you like. Work at a slow to moderate level of activity, so you don't strain muscles. Once you feel loose and warm, you're ready to stretch.

1. Hamstring stretch. Keep your legs straight and your back flat. **2. Calf stretch.** Straighten one leg at a time and feel a gentle pull along each calf. **3. Quadricep stretch.** Push your hips forward for an extra stretch. Keep your knees close together. **4. Lower back stretch.** Slowly rotate your trunk.

Stretching exercises

Hold each of the following stretches for 20 seconds and repeat each stretch twice.

- **Hamstrings.** Stand with your feet together and bend over to touch your toes. Keep your legs straight but not locked. Keep your back straight rather than curved; to do so, lift your head slightly and look up toward your eyebrows.

- **Calves.** Support your body with your hands and the balls of your feet. Straighten one leg at a time and feel a gentle pull along each calf.

- **Quadriceps.** Stand on one leg and pull the foot of the lifted leg to your bottom. Push your hips forward and make sure your knees are next to each other—touching, if possible.

- **Lower back.** Stand with your feet shoulder distance apart. Put your hands on your hips and rotate your trunk in a circle.

I. Regular abdominal crunches.
Keep your head back, and exhale when
you come up. **2. Oblique abdominal
crunches.** Bring your shoulder (not your
elbow) toward the opposite knee. Exhale
as you come up.

Strengthening exercises

Now that you've stretched out, you're ready to really work those muscles.

- **Abdominals.** Many people wake up with a sore back after a day of backpacking
  and assume there is something wrong with their back. In most cases, they just
  need to strengthen their stomach muscles.

    Your lower back is approximately three times stronger than your abdomi-
  nals, yet you only use your back strength when you bend over backwards. All
  forward bends rely on your abs to support your upper body and trunk.

    You can improve the strength of your abs by doing simple crunches on
  the floor. A 30-minute abs aerobics class is ideal, if you have access to one. If
  not, do crunches until your muscles burn. This *is* fun. Take a short break and do
  crunches that work the sides of your stomach, your obliques. Crunch from side
  to side and do as many repetitions as you can. Many weight exercises should be
  done every other day so you don't overstress certain muscles. Abs, however, are
  an exception; it is beneficial to work your ab muscles every day.

- **Calves.** Improving the strength of your major muscle groups will ultimately
  improve your endurance. Start with your calves. Stand on a step with your
  heels hanging off. You may want to hold onto a railing or wall for balance.

Calf raises. Lift your body weight onto your toes; then slowly lower yourself down so your heels hang below the step.

Squats. 1: Keep your back straight; don't lean forward. **2:** For an extra challenge, hold a milk jug filled to a desired weight.

Lift your body weight onto your toes, as high as you can, and slowly lower yourself back down so your heels are hanging below the step. Work up to 30 repetitions, take a short rest, and do another round of 30 repetitions. You do not need to lift extra weights. If it is comfortable on both feet, stand on one foot at a time and increase your reps. Like the abdominal exercises, it is beneficial to work your calves every day.

Glutes and quadriceps. Squats and one-leg lunges work your glutes (butt muscles) and quadriceps (thigh muscles).

Stand with your feet a little more than shoulder width apart. Bend your knees. Keep your back straight and don't lean forward. You'll definitely feel this after a couple squats. Try to do two or three sets of 12 to 15 reps. Rest for 30 to 45 seconds between sets. You want to start the next set before your muscles have completely recovered.

To make this exercise more challenging, hold in front of you a gallon milk jug, filled to the desired weight. Just remember, the more you do now, the easier it will be on the trail.

Now try one-leg lunges. Take a big step forward—a lunge. Make sure that your knee does not extend beyond your toes. Hold this position for a couple seconds

One-leg lunges. Make sure your knee does not extend beyond your toes. You may rest your hands on your thigh, but avoid pressing down. You can also keep your hands on your hips or by your side.

and lunge with the other foot. Again, try to do 30 repetitions before you take a break. Squats and one-leg lunges should be done every other day.

● **Glutes and lower back.** There is another excellent exercise that will strengthen your glutes and lower back. Lie on the floor on your stomach and lift one leg at a time. To make it more challenging, lift both legs at the same time, then lift your upper body as you lift both legs.

Leg lifts. For an extra challenge, raise both legs and upper body.

Upper back exercise. Point your thumbs down and press back. Keep your arms from falling to your sides, even on the last couple presses! Take a break. Then point your thumbs up, and repeat.

1. **Hamstring curls** with ankle weights
2. **Hamstring curls** with surgical tubing

- **Upper back.** You may also want to strengthen your upper back, since those muscles help support the weight of your backpack. From a standing position, hold your arms out so your body looks like a **T**. With your thumbs pointing down, press your arms back 30 times. Take a short rest; then hold your arms out with your thumbs pointing up and repeat the exercise.

You have been using the weight of your body to work your muscles in the previous exercises. But these last two exercises require some additional resistance. Hamstring curls and leg extensions target endurance muscles. If you strengthen these muscles, you'll be backpacking like a pro. You can use ankle weights or a rubber strap such as surgical tubing (which usually sells for about 10 cents a foot at medical supply stores) to add resistance to your muscles.

When doing hamstring curls, stand in front of a counter and hold it for balance. Wearing ankle weights, lift one foot behind you. If you use surgical tubing, tie the tubing around both ankles with an appropriate level of resistance. Do 30 reps, take a 30-second break, and repeat.

For leg extensions, sit on a chair or on the edge of a bed. With ankle weights on, lift one leg straight out in front of you. If you have surgical tubing, tie your ankles together and raise one leg at a time. Do 30 reps for each leg, rest for 30 seconds, and repeat the exercise.

Leg extensions with ankle weights   **Leg extensions** with surgical tubing

Do hamstring curls and leg extensions every other day. When you finish your workout, repeat the stretches outlined on page 28. Stretching will greatly reduce any soreness you may feel the next day.

It is equally important to condition your heart and lungs. Add an aerobic workout to your exercise program. Bike, swim, jog, or walk. If you get your heart rate up for 30 to 45 minutes every other day, you will be on your way to having a more fit body and a more enjoyable trip.

Nutrition

As you get fit for backpacking, eating well is as important as exercise. When you are getting your body prepared for backpacking, it is critical that you maintain healthy eating habits. If you have doubts about what constitutes a healthy diet these days, consult a nutritionist. He or she can analyze your personal eating habits and recommend a diet specific to your body and your needs.

There are some general pointers to keep in mind. First, it is important to eat carbohydrates before you exercise, even if it is just a bagel or a few crackers. You need to make sure that your glycogen reserves are stocked up and ready to fuel your body during the activity. It is equally important to eat carbohydrates within two hours after exercising to maintain a high level of energy. Otherwise you may feel lethargic and get discouraged because 40 minutes of exercise knocked you out for the day.

It is extremely important to drink water. When you are engaged in a rigorous exercise program, you should drink between ten and fifteen cups of water a day. If you do not consume enough water, your body will produce fat more readily—and fat is not going to help you climb any mountains.

MAKING EXERCISE ROUTINE

• • • • • • • • • • • • • • • •

Once you get into the habit of exercising, your workouts will become much easier. Create a schedule for yourself. For example, on Monday, Wednesday, and Friday, do all the strengthening exercises. On Tuesday, Thursday, and Saturday, go swimming, biking, or take a fast-paced walk in your hiking boots and backpack. Then do abdominal and calf exercises. (Remember, the abdominal and calf exercises can be done every day.) Give yourself two weeks of this simple training, and I guarantee you will feel a difference.

Many women find it easier and more motivating to exercise with a friend. Exercising is also easier when it is built into your day. Get into a routine: Do strengthening exercises when you get up in the morning; jog after work or before lunch. It doesn't matter when you do it, as long as you set aside time each day for your exercise program.

The night before a trip, have a big dinner. Many athletes talk about loading up on carbohydrates the night before a big event. While carbohydrates are important, be sure to include protein as well; meat, beans, and peanut butter are good protein sources. It is also a good idea to include fruits and vegetables in your final dinner at home, as the vitamins and minerals found in fruits and vegetables tend to be rapidly depleted and insufficiently replenished on a long hike.

So, you've been strengthening your endurance muscles and improving your cardiovascular condition. You're eating a balanced diet, and you have fueled up the night before your trip. You are prepared for anything. Get a good night's sleep and dream about your upcoming adventure!

OUCHLESS HIKING

The most common backpacking injuries occur to the knees and ankles. You can prevent injuries to those areas by maintaining strong and flexible muscles, by staying in good shape, and by paying attention to where you put your feet.

Exercises

Stretch and strengthen your ankles and knees with the following exercises.

1. **Ankle rotations.** Stand on one foot and rotate the raised foot in a circle.

2. **Calf raises.** Stand on a step with your heels hanging off. This is the same beginning position you used for the calf strengthening exercise. This time, press down on your toes as you raise your heel. In addition to working your calf, you'll also strengthen the top of your foot.

3. Strengthening the muscles around your knee will also help prevent injuries. The exercises for quadriceps, hamstrings, and calves detailed on pages 29–30 and 32 are appropriate.

After you have gotten in shape for your back-packing trip and you are standing in the parking lot ready to begin your hike, take a few moments to stretch out. Remember to warm up first—jog around the parking lot for a few minutes, then stretch your calves, hamstrings, quadriceps, and lower back. Rotate your ankles to loosen them. Now you're ready to hit the trail!

Concentration is key

Most injuries happen after hours of hiking. It's easy to get tired and lose your concentration. When you start tripping over rocks, it's time to take a break. If you are in good shape, you will be less fatigued and reduce the chance of getting injured.

Many injuries to the ankle result from not watching where you're stepping. Hikers often look up at a tree or out to a view and twist an ankle on a rock or root. When you're walking, pay attention to each step. Take scenery breaks to check out the views.

Knee injuries can result if you take a large step up and flex your knee beyond 90 degrees. When you take a large step up, hold onto a tree, a rock, or another person for support. You can also use a hiking stick to take some of the weight off your knees. Hiking sticks are especially helpful on steep descents.

HOW LONG DOES IT TAKE?

Now that you understand what you need to do to physically prepare for a trip, how long will it take to get in shape for backpacking?

The amount of training you endure should depend on the length of your trip and your goals. If you plan to hike five miles, spend the night, and hike out, you may only want to train lightly for two weeks to loosen your muscles. It will take at least two weeks to feel stronger and more fit.

When taking a large step up, don't flex your knee beyond 90 degrees. **1:** Do. **2:** Don't.

For a longer trip, I suggest working through an exercise program for at least six weeks prior the trip. Of course, the longer and harder you train, the better shape you'll be in. If you are in great physical shape, you will feel more comfortable taking a longer or more challenging trip. Often it is more challenging trails that lead to more secluded, less traveled places.

I prepared for two months prior to my Appalachian Trail hike, spending many cold days in December and January hiking a three-mile loop in Valley Forge National Park in Pennsylvania. Often the ground was covered in two feet of snow, so I wore snowshoes and a backpack filled with 20 to 45 pounds of gear and books. People in the park often gave me quizzical looks and asked me where I was going, knowing that in such an urban area I could not possibly be spending the night in our local park. I just smiled and told them that I was training for a long hike. As I kept on, the people got easier to deal with—and so did the terrain. I noticed a remarkable improvement in my speed and endurance in just a few weeks.

If you know you are going on an extended backpacking trip, try to start exercising three months before the departure date. Rate your level of exertion from 1 to 10. If you are sitting and reading, you are probably at Level 1. Level 10 is when you are gasping for air—when you are pushing yourself as hard as you can.

If you train for a trip for three months, you should spend the first month exercising at Level 5 or 6. The second month, raise your exertion level to 7, 8, or 9. During the first three weeks of the third month, you should alternate the level of exertion each day. One day, stay at Level 3. The next day, work at Level 10. Then, take it easy the week before the trip and stay at Level 3 or 4.

It may take these three months to break in a new pair of boots and feel comfortable wearing a pack. Three months will give you adequate time to get in shape, assemble gear, familiarize yourself with your equipment, organize your food, and plan the route you'd like to hike. As you get in better shape and become more familiar with your gear and various hikes, you will need less time to plan your trip.

Chapter 4

EQUIPMENT

CHOOSING AND BUYING GEAR

You don't have to become a "gearhead" to enjoy a backpacking trip. But to tell you that it doesn't matter what gear you use would be a dreadful mistake. Boots, backpacks, tents, and sleeping bags come in hundreds of makes and models. Beyond the essential items, there are dozens of luxury items such as espresso makers and stove stands that an experienced backpacker would never consider lugging along. Deciding what gear will suit your needs can be a challenge, and walking into an outfitting store can be overwhelming—unless you know what you are looking for before you enter.

The only way to know if you like a piece of equipment is to use it, and one option is to test gear before you buy it. Most outdoor outfitters and many university outing clubs rent gear for a minimal price. This is an excellent way to experiment with different brands and styles and to make sure you really enjoy backpacking before you shell out money for your own equipment.

Another way to cut costs is to make your own equipment. If you have a knack for sewing and constructing things, you may want to buy your own materials and make your own backpack, tent, or clothes. Clothes may be the easiest to make, and doing so can save you hundreds of dollars.

Many women make their own fleece jackets, vests, and pants. Others sew long underwear out of synthetic material. You can also make little things, such as a water bottle holder fashioned from a bandanna or stuff sacks made of water repellent material. But if you are like me and have trouble sewing on buttons, you may have to purchase your equipment.

There are four major sources of equipment: outdoor outfitting stores, mail order companies, manufacturers' catalogs, and outdoor magazines. The Resource Directory beginning on page 137 provides contact information for many of these organizations.

Outdoor magazines such as *Backpacker* and *Outside* usually include gear reviews in each issue. Each spring, both magazines publish a guide on the latest gear. *Backpacker's Gear Guide* offers an objective look at a wide range of equipment. It is an excellent place to learn about the scope of the equipment, brand names, and price ranges and styles.

Paging through catalogs allows you to browse through equipment choices in the comfort of your home. But when you are ready to buy, I recommend you visit your local outfitter, for two reasons. First, an experienced salesperson can help you make informed decisions and answer your questions on the spot. Second, you can test the gear in the shop before you buy it. Never buy a sleeping bag without laying it on the floor and climbing in. Never buy a backpack without having a salesperson adjust it and fit it to your body. Never buy boots without trying them on and walking around the store. Never buy a tent without setting it up and crawling in. Never buy a stove without lighting it.

When you walk into a store and express interest in a piece of gear, the first question a salesperson will ask is, "What kind of trips are you going to take?" Consider your answer before you enter the store. Where, geographically, are you going to travel and at what time of year? Will the terrain be steep and rugged or level and gentle? Do you plan to hike for a weekend or for weeks at a time?

When you buy gear, consider the quality—how well the item will hold up over time and how well it performs as you test it in the store. While you shouldn't have to raid your bank account, it is true that, generally, the more expensive the gear, the longer it will last. To protect your investment, consider gear that comes with a life-time warranty; manufacturers are usually very good about honoring warrantees.

You should also consider weight. Backpackers are often obsessed with weight, counting to the ounce the weight of their packs. Some take such measures as breaking a toothbrush in half to shed an ounce. When you are out there walking all day, especially late in the day, you too will realize just how important each ounce can be to your overall comfort.

FOOTWEAR

There are many pieces of equipment you can do without, but comfortable footwear is not one of them. Finding the right protection for your feet is essential. You need to wear something that protects and supports your feet and provides good traction. For warm-weather hiking, some people

Approach shoes are an option for short trips on smooth terrain.

Midweight hiking boot. Proper footwear fit is essential to your enjoyment of backpacking.

prefer running shoes with excellent treads; these are often called "approach shoes." For carrying light loads on smooth terrain, approach shoes may be the most comfortable way to go. The majority of backpackers, however, wear hiking boots.

Every backpacker has her own way of categorizing boots. I divide them into four classes: mountaineering, heavyweight, midweight, and lightweight.

A *mountaineering* boot is used for technical ascents, and these boots are designed for rocks, snow, and ice. A *heavyweight* boot is designed to carry heavy loads over long distances. You are likely more interested in a *midweight* boot, which is ideal for light backpacking. They have rigid soles and offer good support, and many of these midweight boots are made from leather or a leather-fabric combination. A *lightweight* boot is designed for day hikes or short backpacking trips when you carry a light load.

A proper fit

When you try on boots, there are a few things you should keep in mind.

First, try on many boots and try them on with wool or synthetic hiking socks. (If you don't have your own socks, the store should provide a pair for you.) Some boot brands run small, some run wide, and many may not come close to fitting your foot. Try a few different brands to find one that best matches the contours of your feet.

Compared to men's feet, women's feet generally are smaller and narrower, with a thinner Achilles tendon and a higher arch and instep. Over the past few years, manufacturers have begun

FOOTWEAR PRICE TAG: WHAT TO EXPECT

You'll discover a broad range of prices within each of the footwear categories.

Boot type	Price range
approach shoes/ lightweight boots	$50–120
midweight boots	$50–180
heavyweight boots	$120–200
mountaineering boots	$200+

to realize that women's feet are different from men's, and many now produce boots designed for women. A good outfitting store will have a separate section for women's boots.

A boot should feel roomy and comfortable. If one of your feet is larger than the other, fit the boot to the larger foot; you can fill the space around the smaller foot by adding an extra insole. Your heel should be snug, but not tight. You should be able to slide your finger between your heel and the back of the boot. Wriggle and curl your toes. If you don't have enough toe room, you may have some very painful descents. The tongue of the boot should fit comfortably across the top of your foot and your foot should fill the volume of the boot. If there is too much or too little room around the instep, have the salesperson make some adjustments or try a different brand.

When you find a pair of boots you are happy with, wear them around the store for at least a half-hour. If they feel good and you decide to buy them, make sure the store has a return policy. If you wear them around your house for a few days and they are uncomfortable, you should be able to exchange them.

Wear your new boots as much as you can before a trip, allowing at least a month to break them in. For my Appalachian Trail hike, I bought a pair of heavyweight boots. Even though I spent three months breaking them in, I suffered from blisters for the first six weeks of my hike! They were far too stiff for me and were likely the wrong brand. When you choose your boots, take time to make the right decision.

Proper care

You have the best chance of keeping your feet dry with a full-grain leather boot. However, as with most types of boots, it is your responsibility to treat the leather to maintain its water repellency. Water repellency treatments come in waxy pastes that you massage into the leather with your fingers or with a cloth, liquids that you paint on, and sprays. Different types of leather and different fabrics require different treatments. For example, if you have Gore-Tex boots, a waxy treatment like Sno Seal will clog the pores in the Gore-Tex. If a product is safe to use on Gore-Tex, it will say so on the label. Ask your salesperson which product is best for your boots.

Caring for your boots can increase their life span tremendously. Clean your boots regularly with a soft brush and store them in a cool, dry place. Excessive dirt can cause leather to harden and crack. Never expose your boots to strong heat sources, such as a radiator or a campfire. Such heat will dry and crack leather, and it can damage fabric boots as well.

When you've worn down the treads, you may want to get your boots resoled. But make sure you replace the soles before the midsoles wear out (the midsole is the shock-absorbing layer between the insole and the tread). Otherwise, resoling may cost as much as buying new boots.

CARRYING THE LOAD: BACKPACKS

Rumor has it, there was a woman who set out to walk the Appalachian Trail with a shopping cart. I can imagine this woman tugging her cart piled with clothes and gear, trying to haul it over rocks and roots, mountain after mountain. I doubt she got very far. I have seen people backpack with duffel bags and rucksacks with no hip belts. If you are a masochist, this may be the way to go. However, manufacturers have worked for years to design a sack that enables a person to carry weight comfortably. They arrived at one solution: the modern backpack.

Internal and external frame packs

There are two basic types of backpacks: those with internal frames and those with external frames.

Internal frame packs fit closely against your back and give you excellent balance and stability. Many proponents of internal frame packs insist they are more comfortable than external frame packs. Internal packs are less bulky, and they are easy to transport in a car trunk or on an airplane and can be stored easily in a tent. An internal frame pack may cost between $200 and $400.

> "I love my backpack! I had a 'unisex' pack for years and couldn't believe the difference when I switched to a woman's model. It made a huge difference in comfort."
>
> —Mandy Williams, age 34

External frame packs, although less popular, are making a comeback. Manufacturers have improved external pack designs, and people are realizing that these new models have many advantages. Because they are rigid and the weight is distributed higher on the pack, you can walk comfortably and in a more upright position on smooth terrain—even with very heavy loads. It is easier to access and organize your belongings. And because the pack sits away from your back, you will stay cooler in hot temperatures. External frame packs are also less expensive than internal frame packs, ranging in price from $100 to $200.

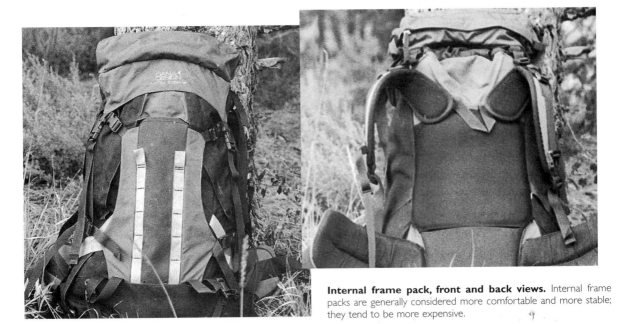

Internal frame pack, front and back views. Internal frame packs are generally considered more comfortable and more stable; they tend to be more expensive.

External frame pack, front and back views. External frame packs allow you to carry a heavy load, provide many pockets, and are less expensive.

PACKS FIT FOR WOMEN

• • • • • • • • • • • • • • • • •

Women's packs are not just smaller versions of men's. The harness on a woman's pack is narrower at the neck and more curved in the chest, and the hip belt flares out more at the hips than the belt on a man's pack. You'll want to try on many packs before choosing, and your pack preference ultimately will boil down to a matter of opinion. However, packs by Dana Designs, Gregory, and Osprey have a reputation for excellence, and their designs seem to fit women well. Most manufacturers now make packs specifically for women.

Proper size and fit

As you shop for gear, rely on your salesperson to help you select the right pack and fit it to your body. This person will be an essential resource; if you sense that he or she has inadequate skill or experience, ask for more help or try another store.

Pack sizes are designated in two ways: volume, expressed in cubic inches; and length, expressed as "small," "medium," or "large" and related to the length of your torso. In terms of volume, you will find packs ranging from a diminutive 2,500 cubic inches to a gargantuan 9,000 c.i. A pack volume of 4,000 cubic inches provides plenty of room for most trips. I prefer a pack with as small a volume as possible: If I have the extra space, I will surely find something to fill it with—and that means I'll carry more weight. If you are not sure how large a pack you need, bring everything you plan to carry on your trip to the store and fill packs of different volumes with your gear (or use gear that is in the store). The second size method will help you find a pack that fits your body. If you have a shorter-than-average torso (the length from the base of your neck to your waist), you'll probably want a size small pack.

Once you have chosen a size you feel is appropriate, load the pack with at least 30 pounds. Even a poorly designed pack can feel comfortable with nothing in it. Put the pack on and cinch the hip belt. The hip belt should rest on your hipbones, not on your waist.

Take advantage of your skeleton—it is built to support weight. The shoulder straps should wrap comfortably around your shoulders. Have the salesperson show you how to properly tighten the shoulder straps. If they are too big or too small, you may be able to replace the harness with an appropriate size. Next, adjust the load lifter straps, which are located next to your ears. When you tighten these straps, more weight is shifted to your shoulders. When you loosen the straps, weight is shifted to your hips.

Finally, clasp the sternum strap across your chest. This strap can be raised or lowered if its current position is not comfortable. Once the pack is fitted, walk around the store for 20 minutes, then try on a different pack and compare how it feels.

Once you've addressed size and comfort, consider what style pack suits you best. Notice where the pockets and compartments are and how the lid attaches to the bag. On some packs, the lid can be transformed into a fanny pack. Some new models have a built-in hydration system so you can suck water through a tube while you walk.

When you buy your pack, it is essential that you buy a pack fly: a piece of water resistant material that fits tightly around the pack to keep it dry in wet weather. Packs are rarely waterproof (only one brand, VauDe, currently offers a waterproof pack), so you will need a fly to prevent all your belongings from getting drenched. Some backpackers take extra precaution by lining their packs with a garbage bag.

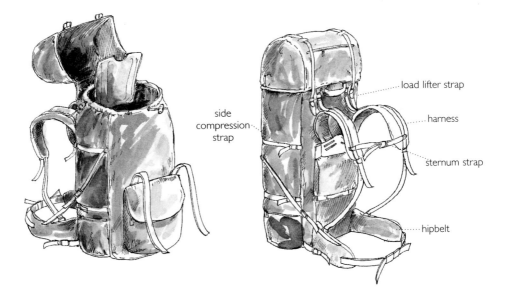

side compression strap

load lifter strap

harness

sternum strap

hipbelt

Pack, including hipbelt, shoulder straps, load lifter straps, and sternum strap.

Proper care

Now that you own a pack, it is important to know how to take care of it. You can treat the pack and fly with a spray that enhances the material's water repellency. Sprays such as Scotch Guard or Tectron are available at your outfitter.

After you use your pack, shake any debris out of the pack and its pockets. Clean the pack with water and a sponge (soaps may break down the polyurethane coating) and air dry your pack. Don't store it while it's damp; mildew will grow and eat through the material.

SHELTER

When you mention wilderness shelter, most people think of tents. But there are alternatives to tents that weigh less and cost less. Of course, these alternatives are not going to perform as well as a tent or offer the same sense of security.

A bivouac bag, or bivy sac, is a water resistant or waterproof shell that slips around your sleeping bag. If you are sleeping alone and don't want to carry the weight of a tent, this may be a good option. It is the best way to feel closest to nature, since you sleep under the stars. Keep in mind, however, that a bivy only provides protection from rain and wind while you sleep. There is no room to sit up, have a drink, or read a book. This can become constricting, especially if you are trying to wait out a long storm. You will not be able to cook or shuffle through your pack without getting wet, and a standard bivy

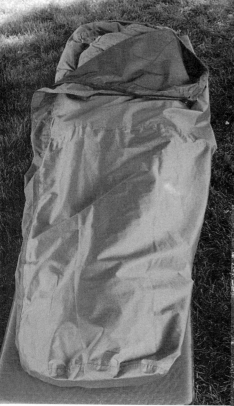

A **bivy sac** is like a shell around your sleeping bag. If you don't mind sacrificing space to minimize weight, a bivy sac is the way to go.

A **tarp** is a lightweight alternative for shelter—but beware the bugs! (Photo by Craig Mills)

offers little protection from biting insects unless the hood is securely fastened over your head. Newer and more expensive models include a small pole that supports the material around your head so you can sit up and read or write and still be protected from rain or bugs.

Few backpackers carry a tarp for shelter, but it is an option. A hardy tarp, if tied and staked properly, can keep you dry. A tarp is a nice supplement to a tent, providing shelter if you are in bear country and need to cook away from your tent. Still, there is nothing to prevent animals like skunks or biting insects from paying you a visit. A strong wind may billow the tarp, and a heavy rain may cause the material to droop and sag.

Choosing a tent

The most reliable and most common shelter is a tent. I'll never go camping without one. Unfortunately, this may be your most expensive purchase. Buying a used tent that is in good condition is one way to save money. It would be ideal to find someone who is upgrading her tent and is willing to sell the old tent to you for a good price.

When you buy a tent, determine if you need a summer tent, a three-season tent, or four-season tent.

A summer tent is best used on desert trips where rain is unlikely. This type of tent has a lot of mesh netting to keep bugs out while allowing maximum ventilation. Most hikers own a three-season tent because they are the most versatile and perform under varied conditions: They insulate on cool evenings, keep you dry during stormy nights, and are well ventilated for warm summer days. But these tents are not designed for winter conditions. If you plan to go winter camping, you need a four-season tent. Four-season tents allow less ventilation, have three or four poles for excellent stability, and have a large vestibule that creates shelter over the doorway. The vestibule is an extension of the rain fly, which is a waterproof layer that fits over the tent to keep you dry in inclement weather. A vestibule can be used as a mud room to store boots and packs out of the rain. It is also good for cooking on rainy days.

After you've selected the appropriate seasonal category, you must determine how many people are going to sleep in the tent.

SHELTER: THE RIGHT CHOICE

• • • • • • • • • • • • • • • • •

It was mid-May and the weather was warming on the Appalachian Trail. My partner and I had been sleeping in a seven-pound Sierra Designs Polaris tent, which worked fabulously during some unseasonably cold and snowy conditions. In Virginia, though, we felt we could do better. We found a three-pound teepee and proclaimed ourselves geniuses. We had just cut the weight of our tent by over 50 percent!

The first few nights were mild and the teepee worked fine. Then it rained. Water flowed down the dip in front of the floorless teepee and into our sleeping space. Angry gusts of wind spanked the sides of the tent and billowed the material. It barely held. Within a week, baby biting flies emerged in swarms. Our teepee was a nightmare. We had nowhere to hide—the sides of the tent were six inches off the ground. We cursed the flies, the teepee, and ourselves for being so foolish. We got our old tent back as soon as we could.

The **three-season tent** is a versatile and popular shelter choice.

More often than not, if a tent is classified as a two-person tent, it is barely big enough for two people. If you want to sprawl out at night, I suggest getting a tent designed for one more person than is in your group. Of course, larger tents are heavier and more expensive, but a good night's sleep may be well worth it.

Make sure your salesperson shows you how to pitch the tent in the store. Sprawl out in the tent and make sure it is an appropriate size and has the features you are looking for.

Finally, before you buy, consider two additional factors: color and weight. Bright colored tents stand out in photographs, but they may also be a form of visual pollution. I once had a bright yellow tent pitched on the shores of a rippling, mountain lake. Late in the afternoon, I was asked by a ranger to move it into the woods. My tent was an eyesore to hikers passing by the lake. As always, weight is a factor. If you have narrowed your choice down to a few acceptable choices, I would go with the lightest one.

Tent with vestibule. The rain fly extends over the door to create a small space for cooking or storing gear.

In addition to the rain fly, a ground cloth will help keep your tent dry. It will also protect the floor of your tent from punctures or tears. A ground cloth is a piece of material shaped like the floor of your tent. It usually clips or straps onto the tent; however, if your ground cloth does not attach and just sits beneath the tent, it is important to make sure the cloth does not extend beyond the tent floor. If your ground cloth is larger than the floor of the tent, it will collect water that runs off the tent walls, and a pool will form beneath you. The best option is a ground cloth made to fit your tent, but you can also cut a piece of plastic or an old shower curtain to fit your tent.

Maintaining your tent

To expand the life of your new tent and keep it functioning well, follow some general maintenance guidelines.

Most tents come with seam sealer. If not, purchase a tube of it. Seam sealer prevents water from seeping in through the seams. Set up your tent at home and put the fly on inside out. Apply seam sealer to all the seams on the fly and to the seams around the base of the tent. Apply the seam sealer to the shiny side of the material. Let seam sealer dry overnight before putting your tent away.

When you put your tent back in the stuff sack, stuff it in bunches. If you fold a tent every time you store it, creases can form and crack the waterproofing material. Never pack your tent if it is wet, unless you have to. If you must travel with a wet tent, shake off as much water as you can. When you do get to a dry place, set the tent up immediately and let it dry out.

Don't expose your tent to direct sunlight for long periods. UV rays can deteriorate the fabric.

After every trip, set your tent up and let it air dry. Even if it didn't rain, your tent may be damp from condensation. Never store a wet tent for an extended period of time. Mildew will surely grow and eat holes in the material, and there is no way to get rid of mildew.

Keep your tent clean by shaking debris out of it before you pack it up. You can wash a tent with a cloth and water and mild soap. Many harsher soaps will break down the waterproof coating.

FOR A SOUND SLEEP: SLEEPING BAGS AND MATTRESS PADS

Selecting a sleeping bag is easier than choosing boots, a backpack, or a tent, simply because there are fewer choices.

You may already have a sleeping bag tucked away in a crawl space or in your attic. I used to have a rectangular, cotton bag with jungle designs all over it. My brother's bag was decorated with

Star Wars figures. There was a time when these worked fine for us. We'd set our bags on bulky, yellow egg-crate pads and camp out in the backyard.

But if you are going to be a serious backpacker, this system will not work. Cotton bags are not warm on cool evenings, and they become waterlogged if they get wet. Most bags today are mummy bags, named for their shape: they are narrow and taper toward the bottom to keep you warmer and reduce their weight.

Choosing a sleeping bag

There are two major decisions when selecting a sleeping bag: Should you buy a bag filled with down or with a synthetic material; and how warm a bag do you need?

Mummy bag. When choosing a sleeping bag, keep in mind the conditions you are most likely to encounter. (Photo by Stacy Middleton)

Down bags are lighter, more compact, and more comfortable than their synthetic counterparts. Unfortunately, they are also more expensive, more difficult to clean, and impossible to deal with when wet. Synthetic bags are heavier and bulkier, but they are less expensive and easier to clean. They also maintain some of their warming qualities if they get drenched. Some of the new synthetic fills are lighter and less bulky than before, and these new fills rival down.

I have one of each type. I use an inexpensive synthetic bag for extended trips where my bag will take its share of abuse, and I use a warmer, down bag for short trips when the temperatures are likely to be low.

Now consider the temperature rating of your sleeping bag. All bags list the lowest temperature at which the bag should keep you warm. Of course, this varies tremendously between individuals.

The type of tent you have, the type of sleeping pad, the clothes you wear, your metabolism, and what you had to eat and drink all affect how warm you will be when you sleep. I am a very cold sleeper and need a sleeping bag with a rating lower than the lowest temperature I expect to encounter. A 15- or 20-degree sleeping bag will serve you well for most three-season trips. If you travel only in the heat of summer or in the desert, you may want a 40- or 50-degree bag. If you camp in the winter, you may need anywhere from a 0- to a –20-degree bag.

Any bag should have a couple of key features. Your new bag should have a hood, one equipped with a drawstring so you can close the hood tightly around your head in cold weather. Most bags have a two-way zipper so you can stick your feet out on warm nights. The bag should come with its own stuff sack. A down-filled bag should come with a storage sac. You can often choose which side of the bag you prefer the zipper on. If you and your significant other buy sleeping bags with opposite zippers, you may be able to zip them together and create one big bag.

Sleeping bags often are sized as short, regular, or long. If you are not very tall, it makes sense to get a short bag so you don't have to carry the extra length that you won't use. Your bag should taper to your shins and provide a little extra room at your feet in case you need to store a camera or contact lenses on a freezing-cold night.

Manufacturers are beginning to make bags specifically for women. Sierra Designs and The North Face make a variety of women's models. LaFuma America and EMS also make bags to fit women's bodies.

> "My first sleeping bag was rated –10 degrees. It was a gift, so I couldn't complain. But it was so bulky it took up half my pack, and it weighed a ton. When I finally scrounged enough money to buy a +20 degree bag I couldn't believe the difference! It was easy to carry and far more comfortable on summer trips. These bags may look the same but there's a world of difference when you climb inside."
>
> —Nancy Hillerman, age 42

Caring for your sleeping bag

As with your other equipment, it is important to know how to care for your sleeping bag. You should never store a bag in a stuff sack. This can compress the fill to such a point that it won't fluff up again, drastically reducing its ability to keep you warm. Many bags come with a roomy storage sack, and you can also lay your bag on a shelf or over a hanger.

Dirt and body oils can eventually work their way into the fill, so try to keep the inside of your bag as clean as possible. Change into camp clothes before you slip into the bag. If it's warm enough, rinse off before bed. You can put a synthetic bag in a front-loading washing machine or wash it by hand with a mild soap. Dry a synthetic bag in a dryer on low heat or lay it across several clothes lines. Don't wash a down bag unless you absolutely have to, since down loses some of its insulating properties every time it's washed.

The time will come, however, when you can't bear to spend another night in your bag unless it's cleaned. Down bags should be washed by hand in a bathtub and dried in a dryer. It is unwise to dry clean any sleeping bag, as most chemicals will strip away down's natural oils and destroy synthetic fibers. However, some dry cleaners can clean down with a special cleaner called Stoddard Solvent.

In the field, shake your down bag and fluff it up before you go to bed. This will increase the loft and keep you warmer. Every morning, allow the moisture in your bag to evaporate before you pack it up. Even if it hasn't rained, moisture from your body will have dampened your bag in the night.

Mattress pads

You may want to add a mattress pad for your sleeping comfort. Mats provide a soft layer between you and hard, rough ground and provide insulation from cold.

There are two main types of mattress pads: closed-cell foam mats and self-inflating mattresses. The foam mats are much less expensive than the self-inflating pads, and they are typically lighter. Foam mats, however, are bulky and less comfortable. The tremendous comfort of the self-inflating pads (such as the brand Therm-A-Rest) is reflected in their prices. Prices also vary, depending on thickness, length, and width. Some pads are two inches thick and unfold to the full length of your body. Others are very thin and may cushion only the area from your shoulders to your hips. If you choose a self-inflating mattress, you should also get a patch kit in case you get a hole in the mattress along the way.

Self-inflating mattress (left) and foam mat (right).

The best way to select your sleeping equipment is to lie down in the store in a sleeping bag on top of a mattress pad. Only you will be able to decide how much comfort and cushion you need. Of course, the larger the pad, the bulkier and heavier it will be to carry. I personally think that a comfortable sleep is worth a little extra weight.

Proper maintenance of your mattress pad will increase its life and keep you sleeping soundly for many nights on the trail. Wipe dirt off your pad after every trip. Store a self-inflating mattress unrolled with the valve open, and lay a foam pad under your bed or on a shelf.

WILDERNESS WEAR

It is very easy to pack too many clothes for a backpacking trip. Since every ounce counts, you want to make sure that you use every item you bring. Changing clothes every day, or a couple times a day, is a luxury—and it is not necessary. Trust me, you will do fine wearing the same outfit every day.

It doesn't matter what brand of clothes you wear, as long as each item fits properly and does its job. The Wild Rose brand offers backpacking clothes and equipment specifically for women.

Backpackers have thought long and hard about the lightest, warmest, and most efficient wilderness clothing. The most popular way to dress for backpacking is layering, using several lightweight layers that can be easily shed.

Start with the undergarments. Your underwear and bra can be made of any material besides cotton. Many sports bras are made from nylon and have lots of mesh so your skin can breathe.

Next is the long underwear layer. These garments should be lightweight, synthetic, and able to wick moisture away from your skin. Remember: Never wear cotton for hiking; it holds water close

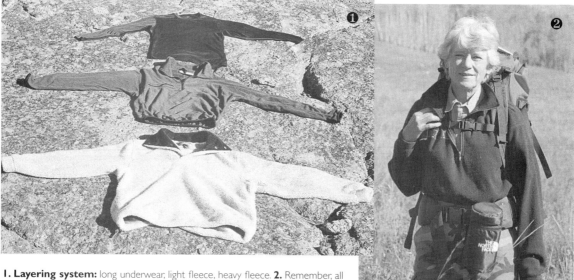

1. Layering system: long underwear, light fleece, heavy fleece. **2.** Remember, all these layers should be made of synthetic materials. (Right photo by Maureen Hall)

to your body and sticks to your skin, reducing the air space around your body. It is this air pocket that keeps you warm.

The next layers on your upper body should consist of a lightweight fleece or wool garment followed by a heavy fleece jacket or wool sweater. If you don't own any fleece or wool garments, you may want to visit a thrift store—you may be able to find these materials for a lot less money than if you bought them new.

Top your layers off with a waterproof shell. Gore-Tex jackets are the most waterproof items on the market.

Waterproof jacket. Gore-Tex is the most popular waterproof jacket material. (Left photo by Donna Middleton, right photo by Maureen Hall)

They are breathable, durable, and also ridiculously expensive. In my experience, if it pours, you get wet no matter what you are wearing. Plus, the fabric is breathable but not *that* breathable: My Gore-Tex jacket never allowed more than a drop of rain to reach my body, but I was drenched from my own perspiration from backpacking in Gore-Tex.

One alternative to Gore-Tex, or to getting soaked in a storm because a cheap rain jacket can't hold up, is to bring an umbrella. When I first saw a backpacker with an umbrella, I laughed and commented how silly it was. Then I noticed that this person was completely dry, and I was hot and wet. Of course, this won't work well if you are on a windy ridge. But if the wind isn't too

"**I** remember one night in the White Mountains of New Hampshire. Two guys arrived at our shelter, wet and shivering. They didn't have rain flies, so everything they had was drenched. Their sleeping bags were soaked! To top it off, they were wearing cotton. Someone offered them a couple of dry fleece jackets and made sure they had enough to eat. Still, I don't know how they made it through the night. I remember being so thankful that I saved a dry set of clothes."

—Patty Mills, age 36

Baggy shorts, synthetic wicking shirt. Save the cotton for camp! (Photo by Maureen Hall)

strong, an umbrella can be secured to your backpack, freeing your hands and sheltering you and your pack from the rain.

Back to the layers for your bottom half. On top of your long underwear you may want to wear insulating pants, such as those made from fleece. If it's not too cold you won't need the extra insulation, and you may want to wear shorts or light trail pants instead. Make sure you bring a pair of light rain pants. They can serve as camp pants to wear on cool evenings and can protect your legs from biting insects.

If the temperature ranges from warm to hot, you should still bring long underwear and light rain gear, but substitute the fleece and wool for T-shirts and shorts. Some women who have mastered the skill of peeing standing up recommend very baggy shorts so you can slide a leg aside and relieve yourself without having to take your pack off. You can wear a cotton T-shirt if it is a scorcher, but wet cotton can be incredibly annoying as it sticks to your skin all day. I recommend a wicking, quick-drying, synthetic T-shirt or tank top. Save the cotton to wear around camp—you can't beat the comfort.

Wear the same hiking clothes every day and save a clean shirt and socks to wear around camp and during the night. When you rise the next morning, it is very important to change into your dirty hiking clothes. If you wear your clean clothes, they will get dirty and wet in a couple hours. Then you will have nothing to change into that evening.

I always bring a warm hat, even in the summer. I often get chilled after stopping for the day, and a hat is the perfect piece of clothing to warm me up. Gloves are another must. If there is a chance of encountering cold, wet weather, bring a waterproof glove shell so your hands don't get wet and numb. Putting a plastic baggy over your hands will act as a vapor barrier and will serve the same purpose as an expensive waterproof shell.

If there is any item that you don't want to skimp on, it is socks. Hiking socks should be a wool/nylon or wool/polypropylene combination—never cotton! Wear silk, olefin,

Gaiters are a must for keeping debris and water out of your boots.

or polypropylene sock liners beneath your beefy hiking socks to help prevent blisters. You may want to change your socks during the day or alternate your dirty socks every other day. If it is warm, you can rinse your socks out each evening and dry them on your pack the next day. Keep one pair clean and dry at all times so you'll always have a pair to change into.

To help keep your socks dry, you may want to wear gaiters. These handy devices wrap around your leg from your ankle to your knee and prevent water and debris from entering your boots. They also protect your legs from getting scraped as you walk past prickly brush. Shorter ankle gaiters are cooler for walks in the summer.

A bandanna is another excellent accessory and one that I bring on trips in all seasons. Because of the big push to get away from cotton, I found that I had nothing to soak up water. I wanted to dry off my face and body, blow my nose, and keep perspiration from dripping into my eyes—a bandanna was the perfect solution. Wearing a wet bandanna on your head can cool you off, and wearing one sheik-style to cover your ears and neck can be a blessing in mosquito infested areas.

It is critical that you keep your clothes in a water-resistant stuff sack. Dry clothes are not just a luxury; your survival could depend on them.

Maintain a material's water resistance by washing it with a treatment such as Nikwax's TX Direct. You can wash Gore-Tex in a machine and dry it on low heat, but dry cleaning it will ruin its water repellency. Ironing Gore-Tex reconditions the fabric and improves its repellency.

Chapter 5

TRICKS OF THE TRAIL

BEFORE YOU GO: PACKING YOUR PACK

You cross a ridge and get hit with a sudden thunderstorm. You and your gear get drenched for five minutes while you dig through your pack to locate your rain coat and pack fly.

You descend into a marsh, and mosquitoes swarm your body. You're eaten alive as you frantically search for repellent and a long-sleeve shirt.

You're hiking the final mile of the day in the dark. Suddenly, your flashlight goes out, and you can't remember where you put the spare batteries.

Sound scary? You can avoid all these scenarios if you have a well-organized pack. How you pack your belongings depends largely on whether you have an internal or external frame backpack. Because external frame packs have many small pockets and lots of room to secure items outside the pack, hikers with external frame packs organize their gear differently than those with internal frame packs (which typically have one large compartment and one small top pouch).

If you have an internal frame pack, put your sleeping bag in the bottom of the pack. Your sleeping bag is a bulky item that is hard to squeeze in anywhere else. It's smart to keep things at the bottom of your pack that you won't need during the day. I have an internal frame pack, and I like to put food and clothes that I won't need that day on top of the sleeping bag. If you can't fit everything in, use STRAPits (elastic straps that sell for about four dollars) or bungee cords to secure equipment on the outside of the pack; be sure, though, to attach only things you wouldn't mind getting damp, dirty, or crushed. A sleeping mattress or a tent is a good choice.

On an external frame pack, strap your sleeping bag under the main compartment and a tent or a sleeping mattress above the main compartment. Fill the bottom of the main compartment with items that you may not need during the day.

No matter what type of pack you have, keep frequently used items—such as your water purification, a warmer top, and snacks—in places that are easy to access. I usually keep my journal, first aid kit, and pack fly in the top pouch. A rain storm can appear out of nowhere, and you may need to access rain gear quickly. Also, keep your fuel bottle away from your clothes and food—there are few things worse than fuel-soaked food! You may want to attach the fuel bottle outside your pack to prevent a catastrophe in case of a leak.

Some women backpackers suggest putting heavy items at the bottom of the pack and toward your back to keep your center of gravity low. Others suggest carrying heavy items high in your pack and toward your back. It may be more comfortable to walk with more weight at the top, but you might lose stability and balance. Experiment with different ways of loading your pack and find out what works for you.

Some hikers organize groups of gear in different colored stuff sacks. These durable, water-repellent bags make it easier to locate an item without having to empty your entire pack. For instance, if you put all your clothes in a blue stuff sack, you'll know just where to look when you need a warmer top. Put anything that you don't want to get wet in a Ziploc freezer bag and bring an extra in case one rips. You may also want to wear a small fanny pack in front of you. It's nice to have a snack, your maps, lip balm, and a camera within your grasp so you don't have to take off your backpack. Also, make sure your water is within easy reach.

Your loaded pack (including food) should weigh between one-fourth and one-third of your body weight. If you can get it lower than that, you are an exceptionally good packer. For longer trips and trips in cold weather, your pack may weigh more because you'll be carrying more food and special cold weather gear—extra clothes, snowshoes, or crampons (ice cleats). On a desert hike, it may be necessary to carry a couple days' worth of water. This can increase

External straps secure items outside your pack.

Mount your pack by first resting it on your thigh, then swinging it onto your shoulders.

your pack weight tremendously. On some trips, a pack that weighs 40 percent or more of your body weight can't be avoided.

After you've loaded your pack and stared at it in disbelief, wondering how you are ever going to carry it, try to mount it without straining yourself. Lunge forward and lift your pack so it rests on your thigh. Slip one arm into the harness, swing your pack onto your shoulder, and put the other arm through. Then clasp the hip belt and tighten the straps. If you can't mount your pack by yourself, it's a good indi-

cation that you overpacked. Unpack, reconsider taking certain items, and reload.

ON THE TRAIL

Finding your way

You won't have trouble finding your way on many trails. The path is usually worn down and well defined. Trails are often marked with signs; some show mileage to upcoming destinations, such as road crossings, the next pass, or a campground. Some trails are blazed, which means trees or rocks along the trail are painted with a colored stripe of paint. Trees that have two blazes indicate a turn. If the top blaze is positioned slightly to the right of the bottom blaze, make a right turn. In place of blazes, other trails have colored metal circles or triangles tacked to trees. Follow the markings and you will find your way.

Trails above treeline may be more difficult to follow. These trails are usually marked with piles of rocks, called *cairns*. From one cairn you should be able to spot the next one and walk toward it. Following these trails may become more difficult in snowy conditions, as cairns may be buried and blazes hidden. I sometimes find myself asking, If I were a trail, where would I be? During those times, a map can be quite handy!

It is important to carry a map and compass even on the most well defined trails, because other paths may bisect your trail. When you're in the woods, you don't want to have the slightest doubt about which path is the correct one. It only takes one error to throw you off course. Maps also indicate water sources. The location of water is critical for planning rest stops, meals, and where to spend the night. It's much easier to look on a map for a splash of blue than it is to roam the woods in search of water.

There are two types of maps to help you find your way: planimetric maps and topographic maps. *Planimetric* maps represent features on the ground. *Topographic*, or topo, maps show how the ground is shaped. The contour lines on topo maps connect areas of similar elevation. The distance between each contour line may represent a distance of 15 to 500 feet, depending on the map. Your map will include a scale to tell you what contour interval it uses.

Two blazes indicate a turn. A right turn is pictured here.

When the contour lines are spaced far apart on a topo map, there is only a slight change in elevation, or a gradual slope. When the contour lines are very close together, there is a steep slope. If the lines are touching, there is a cliff. By examining a topo map, you can tell how steep a climb is and how many feet you must ascend, where the trail crosses a water source, and what land forms surround you.

The National Park Service and the National Forest Service are good sources for acquiring planimetric maps. The

Cairns are piles of rocks that mark the trail above the treeline.

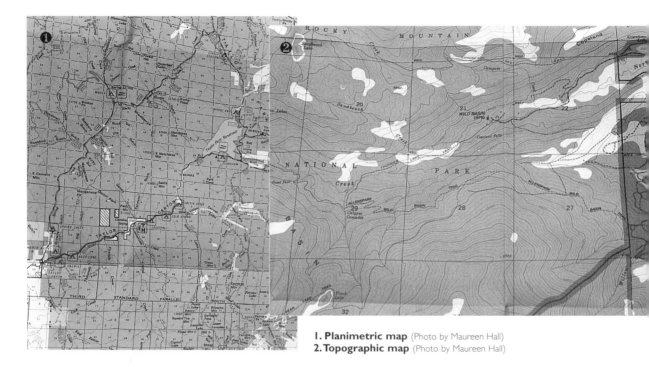

1. **Planimetric map** (Photo by Maureen Hall)
2. **Topographic map** (Photo by Maureen Hall)

• •

"**A** friend and I were hiking in northern Michigan and decided to try to find our way to the next lake using a map and compass. We had practiced in my backyard but had never tested our skills in the field. We set a bearing and checked our progress often. When we found the right lake, we couldn't believe it! I guess neither of us thought we really had the skills to do it, but we did!"

—Mandy Williams, age 34

• •

United States Geologic Survey and some private companies like Trails Illustrated, Earthwalk Press, and Wilderness Press make topographic maps. (See the Resource Directory, page 137, for addresses.)

Map and Compass

If you stick to well marked trails, you may never need to use a compass. But what if you make a wrong turn or you want to double-check the accuracy of a sign? What if there is a rock slide that you have to navigate around to reconnect with the trail? What if there is an emergency and you need to take a shortcut out of the woods? What if you don't want to stick to the trails and prefer a cross-country experience? As you become a more experienced backpacker, these situations become more likely, so it's a good idea to have a compass and be familiar with basic navigation techniques.

You don't need a fancy compass: An inexpensive, plastic, standard compass will do.

In the following section, I'll take you through three basic map and compass exercises. It helps immensely to have a map and compass in front of you as you work through these! If you want to learn more about orienteering, you can get involved with orienteering clubs and classes. Orienteering is actually a sport where participants race to find certain checkpoints using a map and compass. There are also plenty of books on the subject; some great ones are listed in the "Get going and get back" section of the resource directory, page 137.

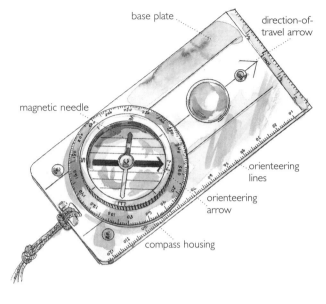

Basic compass

I know where my destination is, but I don't know how to get there

This sounds a little strange at first, but let's say your goal is to make it to a lake. From the overlook where you're standing, you can see the lake in the next valley. But as you descend, you know the lake will be out of view. Use a compass to set a bearing so you will know which direction to travel in, even when you can't see your destination.

Bearings are given as degrees. To set a bearing, point the direction-of-travel arrow at your destination. Turn the compass housing until the red end of the magnetic needle is aligned with the orienteering arrow. Think of the phrase "red in the shed" to remember which part of the needle to focus on. Keep these two arrows pointing north and follow the direction-of-travel arrow until you get to the lake. In most cases you will want to aim for a checkpoint along the way. Head toward an enormous tree or other landmark on the ridge, then check your bearing and head for the next checkpoint.

Align the magnetic needle with the orienteering arrow. (Photo by Craig Mills)

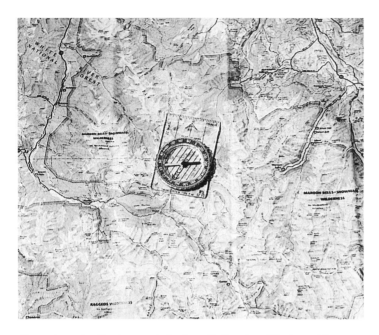

Connect your location to your destination with the edge of the base plate.

I know where I am, but I don't know where my destination is

A time may come when you have a good idea where you are, but you don't know which direction to travel in to get to your destination. If this is the case, you need to take a bearing off your map.

Locate where you are on the map. Then connect your location to your destination with the edge of the compass's base plate. Rotate the compass housing until the orienteering arrow is aligned with north on the map. Take the compass off the map and turn it, without rotating the housing, until the magnetic needle and orienteering arrow are aligned. Note your bearing and follow the direction-of-travel arrow to your destination.

When you are orienteering with a map and compass, you must account for magnetic variation. *Magnetic north*, which is located in northern Canada and is where the compass needle points, is different from *true north*, which is located at the North Pole. The earth's magnetic force pulls a compass needle out of line with true north. Because magnetic north changes every year, mapmakers use the consistent true north, instead. The difference between magnetic and true north is measured as an angle called *magnetic variation*, or declination.

In parts of Michigan, Indiana, Ohio, Kentucky, Tennessee, North Carolina, and South Carolina, magnetic north and true north coincide. In states farther east, true north is west of magnetic north. In states west of the above mentioned states, true north is east of magnetic north.

The legend on your map should tell you how many degrees difference there is between magnetic and true north, and also how many degrees it changes each year. For example, you are using a 1996 map that tells you the declination in that area is 15 degrees west and moving 2 degrees east each year. That means that in 1998 the declination should be 11 degrees west.

If your map doesn't give the declination, you can calculate it your-

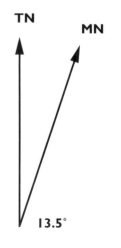

The magnetic declination is 13.5 degrees.

self. Using your compass, take a bearing from your position to a landmark. Then take a bearing to the same landmark using your map. To do this, align the compass with the landmark on the map; turn the compass housing until the orienteering arrow is facing north on the map. The difference between the two bearings is the declination. You may want to mark the declination on your compass to save yourself from having to calculate it more than once—unless you travel to a different location.

Now, when you take a bearing from a map, add the declination to the bearing if you are in the Eastern states and subtract the declination from the bearing if you are in the Western states. Now that you have your adjusted bearing, follow the direction-of-travel arrow to your destination.

I don't know where I am

Okay, so you're lost—let's say "temporarily displaced." If you can locate two landmarks and find them on the map, you can use a map and compass to estimate your location. This technique is called *triangulation.*

Set the dial on the compass to north and lay the compass on the map with the direction-of-travel arrow pointing to magnetic north. Turn the map and compass together until the red end of the magnetic needle is pointing to zero degrees on your compass. The map now faces true north.

Take the compass off the map and point the direction

Triangulating your position using two landmarks. (Photo by Craig Mills)

of-travel arrow toward a landmark. Rotate the dial until the red end of the magnetic needle points to zero degrees and read the bearing. Now, put the compass back on the map with the edge of the compass touching the landmark. Turn the entire compass until the orienteering lines on the compass are parallel with magnetic north. Make sure the edge is still touching the landmark. Draw a line along the edge of the compass that crosses the landmark. Repeat the process with a second landmark. Your location is at the intersection of the two lines. Now you can be on your way.

"**I** like to travel at a slow to moderate pace. For me, stopping often to look around is what backpacking is all about. It is important to travel with people who have similar goals, though, or you'll end up frustrated with one another."

—Laurie Ehlers, age 29

Finding your pace

Some backpackers like to race to their destination and then relax all afternoon at their campsite, while others travel in short, speedy bursts and rest often. Others walk slowly and steadily and spend most of the day getting to their destination. Each of these methods is fine. Find your own rhythm and develop a pace that is comfortable for you.

I like to start out slow and get into a groove. As my breathing becomes steadier, I increase my speed. If you gradually increase your heart rate, your breathing will plateau. I found that if I go too hard too fast, I gasp for air and need to stop more frequently. Especially on the uphills, it is important to pay attention to your breathing. Inhale through your nose, exhale through your mouth. Concentrate on listening to your breaths, not on the strain in your legs. Match every step, or every second or third step, with a breath. Put yourself in low gear and you will be at the top in no time.

If you are traveling with a partner or group, you may want to speed up or slow down in order to stay together. Or you can decide on a resting spot and agree that each person will travel at her own pace to get there. Don't leave anyone behind and don't let your group leave you in the dust.

If the group includes people of varied abilities, allocate the weight each member must carry. Give the most fit person the heaviest load. This will help average out the pace of the group so you all can stay together. Again, if you decide to separate from a partner or a group, agree ahead of time where you are going to reconvene. Never leave a group without carrying ample water, food, and shelter. If your partner is carrying the tent, you should carry the ground cloth or rain fly.

If you bring a watch, time yourself to see how many miles you walk in an hour. If you travel at 2 miles per hour and you know that you need to travel 10 miles, you can plan your day knowing that you must spend five hours walking. The terrain and slope can affect your pace, but all the ups and downs usually average out.

Steep terrain

At some point in your backpacking adventures you may have to travel down a steep slope or down a slope of loose rock or dirt. You don't have to crawl down if you know how to descend safely.

There are three ways to get down on your feet. The first method involves turning sideways and stepping with your knees bent. If you'd rather

"**W**hen I'm having trouble on steep, slippery descents or I'm scared about being close to a narrow ledge, I just think of that little engine . . . 'I think I can, I think I can, I think I can . . .'"

—Elizabeth Fox, age 55

Three ways to safely descend. 1: Turn sideways and step with your knees bent. **2:** Dig your heels into the earth. **3:** Flex your ankles and walk down slowly. (Photos by Craig Mills)

approach the hill straight on, you can dig into the earth with your heels. The third technique involves flexing your ankles and walking down slowly. Make contact with the earth with your entire foot. One thing to remember when using any of these techniques is to keep your weight forward. If you don't, the weight of your pack will pull you back, and you may find yourself sliding down on your bottom. This is always an option, but not a comfortable one!

You may find it easier to walk both down and up steep terrain if you use a hiking stick. Use a staff to brace yourself on the way down, to add extra balance and support, and to take some of the weight off your knees. A narrow tree limb, a ski pole, or a trekking pole are also handy when you are hiking uphill. Put your arms to work! Use the hiking stick to help lift the weight of your body and pack. I prefer to use two poles. That way I get into a rhythm of swinging both arms and take an equal amount of weight off each foot.

Many hikers like to use a small tree limb as a walking stick because it can easily be discarded when no

Use a hiking stick for steep ascents.

FIND YOUR OWN WAY TO CROSS

I was backpacking in Maine during one of the wettest summers in recent history. The rivers had more than jumped their banks—they had devoured them! The trail crossed waterways that were well over my head. Some hikers balanced their backpacks on their heads and bobbed up and down in neck-deep water. No thanks! There was one river I simply could not cross. My partner balanced on a felled tree that was submerged a foot beneath the swift currents, and he made it to the opposite bank. But I was stranded on the other side. I tried to slide across on the log, but all I could think about was falling and getting swept down the river. After a few minutes of tears and frustration, I took out my Therm-A-Rest and began blowing it up. My partner tossed me a rope. I tied the rope to my backpack, held the Therm-A-Rest in front of me, got a running start, and dove into the water. I rafted across as he reeled me in. It may not have been the most graceful way to get across, but what a rush!

Turn slightly upstream when you ford a river. (Photo by Craig Mills)

longer needed. If you carry ski poles or collapsible trekking poles, you can strap them vertically to the outside of your pack when not in use. Collapsible trekking poles fold up to about two feet long, so they're easy to store.

Fording rivers

Many rivers are bridged by wooden slats, logs, or sturdy bridges. However, you may need to cross a river that is not bridged. If the water is low, you may be able to hop across on rocks and stay perfectly dry. If rocks aren't exposed or if the water is high, I suggest wearing sandals or sneakers as you wade across. If you wear your hiking boots, they will be drenched for days. Barefoot crossings are not a good idea either, as bare feet don't get much traction on slippery rocks and have little protection against sharp objects in the stream.

As you approach a river, look for a shallow place to cross that has a slow current. Wider sections of the stream are usually less swift. Rivers are likely to rage after a storm, and many mountain streams are more shallow in the morning before a long day of sunny skies and melting snow.

Before you begin the ford, unclasp your hip belt in case you

● ●

"**W**hen we saw the lake we knew we had to stop and spend the night. The Indian paintbrush and lupines and scarlet gilia were up to my thighs, and the lake was an emerald color I hadn't known water could reflect. We pitched the tent on a bluff overlooking the lake. That evening, the sun glowed pink on the snowy slope that seemed to slide right into the lake. I sat there with a hot cup of tea and basked in the alpenglow. It was one of those moments I hoped would last forever."

—Nancy Hillerman, age 42

● ●

slip in the water and need to quickly take your pack off. Walk slowly with your body facing slightly upstream. Feel the spot in front of you one foot at a time and don't commit your foot until you've found a stable spot. Always use a hiking stick for support. Keep your eyes on your destination: Staring into swirling currents can make you dizzy. If you feel crossing a certain river is too risky, it is better to abandon your route than risk getting seriously hurt.

It is often safer to cross a river in a group. Line up and hold onto each other. Support each other as you make your way across. If there are three of you, form a tripod and navigate the river as a unit. Go slowly and make sure each member is comfortable along the way.

Choosing a camp site

When it's nearing time to choose a place to stop for the night, there are a few things to keep in mind. Most importantly, is there a water source nearby? Your maps should indicate likely water sources. If it looks like the area has been used before, choose a tent site that is already matted down; there is no need to cause further damage to the area. Make sure you choose a site that is at least 200 feet from the trail and the water source. Use existing fire rings and dismantle extras by scattering the rocks and ashes. This will help diminish campers' impact on the environment.

As a general rule, sandy soils or ground covered with pine needles are most comfortable. Find a level space large enough to accommodate your tent, and clear the ground of sharp rocks and sticks. If a slightly slanted patch is the best you can do, keep in mind that you probably want to sleep with your head on the higher side. Now you're ready to pitch the tent and retire for the day. (More low-impact approaches to backpacking are discussed in Chapter 9, page 115.)

AT CAMP

Pitching the tent

It is a delightful feeling to come upon a beautiful place and claim it as your home for the night. I like to set up camp and organize my things right away. After a snack, pitching the tent is usually

my first item of business. All tents are different, so read the instructions for your tent to
learn how to pitch it and practice—before
you head out. It's not a bad idea to also practice pitching your tent in the dark.

Most tents have collapsible poles that
support the dome-shaped material. Lay the
tent on the ground with the floor of the tent
taut. Slide the parts of each pole together
and slip the poles through the fabric sleeves
on the tent. Some tents have loops that the
poles slide through, and other tents have
hooks. After all the poles are in their correct
positions, attach the end of each pole to the
base of the tent by putting them in the
metal-ringed holes. Your tent will pop into
shape. Tip the tent on its side and attach the
ground cloth to the bottom of the tent. If
your ground cloth doesn't attach to your
tent, lay the cloth on the spot where you
want to sleep and then put the tent on the
cloth. (Ground cloths are discussed in more
detail in Chapter 4, page 46.)

Pitching the tent

Make sure the door is facing the direction you want it to face. I like my door to face a nice
view, a lake, or east—so I get the morning sun. When your tent is in position, use a rock to tap
the tent stakes into the ground. If there is a chance of rain, or if you want more insulation, put
the rain fly over the tent and stake it down or clip it to the tent.

Setting up camp in the rain

If you arrive at camp in the rain, you may have to alter your routine. The goal is to organize your
equipment, set up your shelter, eat a meal, and change clothes—all without getting everything
wet. Here's one way to do it.

Remove the tent from your pack and immediately prop your pack against a tree and cover
it with the pack fly. Spread the tent out and put the rain fly on top of it. Make sure you are not
in a drainage area or on the bank of a river that may rise during the night. With the fly covering
the tent, slide the poles through the tent and stake it down. Attach the fly to the tent. Make sure
the rain fly is taut so water can run off, and make sure the fly is not touching the tent. If the fly
rests against the tent material, there is a greater chance that water will seep through. If your tent
has a vestibule, put your pack in the vestibule and lay it on top of its fly so ground water won't

saturate it. From inside the tent, you can arrange your belongings, and everything should stay as dry as can be expected.

If you have a tarp, string it between trees to provide shelter while you cook. If not, move your pack into the tent and use the space in the vestibule to cook. Just remember that synthetic materials—like your clothes, backpack, and the tent—are highly flammable. Keep the flame as far from the tent material as possible. Under no circumstance should you cook *inside* the tent.

Camp chores

When you camp with a partner, you should each have your own camp chores. It works well if you arrive at camp and work together to pitch the tent. Unroll your air mattresses, inflate them and throw in the items you want in the tent: sleeping bags, clothes, a journal, and maps, for example.

One person can then set up the stove while the other gets water. One person cooks the meal while the other purifies drinking water. After you eat, one person can clean the dishes while the other puts the food and stove away. If you get bored with your assignments, switch chores. After a while, you know what needs to be done. When you are exhausted and arrive late to a camp site, it's nice to be able to take care of chores in an efficient manner.

On your first trip, you may need some extra time to figure out what needs to be done. After a couple days, it's easy to get into a routine. If you are traveling with someone or a group, make sure each person has their fair share of the work. And make sure everyone is competent at all the chores. If you like to have different chores, rotate responsibilities every night.

Chapter 6

THE BACKCOUNTRY KITCHEN

APPROACHES TO FOOD

Everyone has her own ideas about food preparation in the backcountry.

Some hikers eat in style. They take hours to prepare multiple courses and don't mind the weight of extra utensils and cooking devices. These gourmet meal makers typically plan their day around food and stop early to prepare a feast. But there are hikers at the opposite end of the spectrum. They sacrifice hot meals for weight; they don't carry a stove, fuel, cookware, cleaning supplies, or a stove repair kit. These items can make a large dent in the weight of your pack. But it is quite a sacrifice to come into camp after a long day and sit down to a dinner of trail mix, bread, and cheese. During cooler months, it can also be dangerous to forgo a hot drink—often one of the only ways to raise your core body temperature.

Stoveless hikers rely on trail mix, health bars, dried fruit, jerky, cheese, bread, and dehydrated meals like rice and peas, which they don't mind eating cold. I have actually seen a person, who apparently had a limited budget and a pitiful understanding of nutrition, survive for weeks on cold Ramen noodles with catsup and Little Debbie Moon Pies (those preserve-saturated oatmeal cookies glued together with marshmallow cream).

I have also seen backpackers live on the expensive freeze-dried meals sold at outfitting stores. These meals are precooked and preassembled. All you do is add boiling water, let it sit for a few minutes, and—voilà!—your beef stroganoff or key lime chicken is ready to eat. Some of these meals actually taste good. But if you're like me and don't have seven dollars to spend on every meal, you will need to come up with your own plan. You don't have to shell out big bucks for freeze-dried food, and you certainly don't have to eat cold Ramen noodles with catsup. With a little planning you can enjoy tasty backcountry meals. Even food prepared by a novice chef tastes like a gourmet meal after a day of hiking.

I used to eat the same meals on every trip: oatmeal for breakfast; instant mashed potatoes and gravy for lunch; flavored pasta for dinner. Then one morning (after eating oatmeal for 33 days in a row), the thought of putting another spoonful of pasty oats into my mouth was enough to make me heave. To this day I avoid oatmeal at all costs. Even if you are incredibly hungry, you may choose hunger over your twentieth lunch of instant mashed potatoes with instant gravy. Diversity of foods is the key to a rich culinary experience.

It is not an easy task to plan your meals for days at a time or even months at a time. When I planned my Appalachian Trail hike, I bought all my food in bulk to save money. I packed the food in boxes and sent it to myself at post offices in towns along the trail. But after a month or two on the trail, I was wondering what I was going to do with the six-month supply of oatmeal, quick-cook rice, and instant mashed potatoes that I no longer wanted to eat. (Of course, I was not the slightest bit concerned about being able to polish off the Snickers and Peanut M&Ms!) I would anxiously await the arrival of the next box of food, in the hope that *somehow* there would be a selection that was different from the previous fifteen boxes! But each time, it was the same old stuff. Sometimes other hikers who were equally disgusted with their new box of food would eagerly trade.

On short trips, it is easy to throw food together at the last minute. However, I urge you not to do this. Take your time and plan your menu. With a little planning and creativity, you can eat tasty and nutritious foods wherever you travel. Whether you prefer a quick, easy approach or a complicated, time-consuming approach, you should base your food selections on nutrition, calories, weight, and packability.

"My favorite backpacking meal is couscous, because it only takes a minute to cook. If I'm feeling more creative, I'll make a resemblance of chicken parmesan: Add a tin of chicken and slices of cheese to pasta and red sauce; throw in a pinch of garlic and a pinch of red pepper. It's quite tasty!"

—Laurie Ehlers, age 29

A balanced diet: carbohydrates, proteins, fats, vitamins, minerals

The first thing to consider when planning your meals is nutrition. Some nutritionists recommend that your backpacking diet consist of 70 percent carbohydrates, 15 percent protein, 15 percent fat, plus a variety of vitamins and minerals.

Carbohydrates should make up the bulk of your diet. Foods such as pasta, rice, potatoes, oatmeal, muesli, fruits, vegetables, crackers, bread, sugars, and honey are considered high in carbohydrates. Sugars provide quick energy, while starches fuel you for the longer haul. It is convenient that many carbohydrates (pasta, rice, oatmeal, cereals, etc.) are lightweight and compact. They also won't spoil, because they are already in a dehydrated state, and they're inexpensive, easy to transport, and simple to prepare.

Protein is essential for backpacking because it helps build muscle and provides your body with energy. Foods high in protein include beans, lentils, meat, eggs, cheese, and peanut butter. You may notice that many of these foods are also high in fat. This is fine; you need fat too. Fat is important since it can be stored and used when you need it. Eating fat at night will give you energy the next morning. Because fat takes three to four hours to digest, as opposed to one to two hours for carbohydrates, you should save the fatty treats until your day's walk has come to an end.

Most of us have no problem getting enough fat. High amounts of fat are found in margarine, cheese, meats, eggs, oils, nuts, peanut butter, and chocolate. A diet consisting of 15 percent fat may be less than you normally consume. On the other hand, if you are extremely health conscious and try to avoid fat altogether, bring the fat back on a backpacking trip. Leave the fat-free foods and diet snacks at home. Foods like fat-free cookies, crackers, and rice cakes tend to have empty calories. Besides, you'd have to fill your entire backpack with rice cakes just to begin to satisfy a backpacker's appetite!

Vitamins and minerals sustain a number of physiological processes, including growth and maintenance of body tissue and the conversion of fat and carbohydrates to energy. Over time, backpackers deplete their reserves of vitamins and minerals because it is difficult to carry nutrient-rich items like fruits and vegetables on a backpacking trip. So you need to make an extra effort. Add dehydrated fruit to oatmeal, trail mix, and health bars. Add dehydrated vegetables to rice, potatoes, and pasta dishes. On weekend trips, you can afford the luxury of fresh fruit. However, longer trips require some foresight. I carry a vitamin and mineral supplement on all trips.

Even more important than a balanced diet is drinking plenty of water. For details on managing your water intake while backpacking, see page 33.

Calorie count: how much food should you bring?

How do you know if you're bringing enough food? As a general rule, it's better to bring too much food than go hungry on the trail. However, there is a difference between bringing an extra day's worth of food and lugging around pounds of food that you can't possibly eat.

When it comes to calories, there is no magic number you should consume. The number of calories you need depends on such factors as your age, weight, metabolic rate, and level of activity. When you are backpacking, your body is working harder than it does in everyday life, so you will need to consume more calories than you usually do. But space in your pack is limited, so you want to carry food that gives you the most calories while taking up the smallest space.

On longer hikes, men often have the problem of losing too much weight and not being able to consume enough calories. Women rarely have this problem because our fat-to-muscle ratio is naturally higher than a man's. We have more energy stored as fat so we don't have to burn muscle for energy. On long-distance trips, it is not uncommon for a man to lose 20 to 30 pounds and for a woman to actually gain a couple pounds due to increased muscle mass. In most cases, women lose some weight, but not as much as men. On my Appalachian Trail hike, I lost 8 pounds while my husband lost 30. Since he knew about the prospect of losing weight, however, he had purposely gained weight before we left.

You can make a rough estimate of how many calories you need. Using the following table, calculate the calories that a 128-pound woman consumes per day on a backpacking trip. Let's say she sleeps and rests for 10 hours (45 × 10 = 450). She reads, sits and talks, draws, or writes for four hours (90 × 4 = 360). She does camp chores for two hours (230 × 2 = 460). She hikes for eight hours (300 × 8 = 2,400). For one day, she needs to consume a total of 3,670 calories.

Average Calories Burned Per Hour (for 128-pound woman)

Activity	Calories per hour
sleeping; resting	30–60
sitting; reading; talking	60–90
writing; drawing; playing cards	90–150
light work; slow walking	120–210
camp chores	180–300
backpacking	240–600

I am 5'7" and weigh 115 pounds. While backpacking, I consume between 2,500 and 3,500 calories a day. On long-distance hikes, when I walk 15 to 20 miles a day, I consume 4,000 to 4,500 calories a day and never feel full for more than an hour.

You may want to count the number of calories you will potentially burn per day and package your food accordingly. If that approach sounds too structured for your style, forget the calculator and simply estimate your portions. If you decide on pasta for dinner, bring the amount of pasta you would eat for a normal dinner at home—whether that's one cup or one pound. Then add a little more. Plan your food this way for a two-day trip, and then go out and see if you hit the mark. If you bring the amount of food you normally eat and supplement it with a little extra pasta for dinner and plenty of snacks you normally don't eat, such as dried fruit and energy bars, you should have plenty of food for your trip.

It is easier to plan for a short trip. If you bring too much food, it's not much of an inconvenience because you're not carrying much food anyway. Things get trickier if you are planning a week-long or month-long trip. If you bring too little food on a long trip, you may have days to walk before you reach a town to resupply. Conversely, if you are carrying food for three extra days, you are going to be carrying an extremely heavy pack. Practice planning for shorter trips first.

There is a delicate balance between the amount and the weight of food. Clearly, the more you carry, the heavier your pack will be, and the heavier your pack, the more energy you'll need to carry it—thus the more food you'll need to consume! The cycle continues. If you carry less food and have a lighter pack, you won't burn as much energy as you would burn carrying a heavy pack. But too little food will make you weak. You will find the right balance with practice.

Plan food for your trip by listing the number of meals you will need. How many breakfasts, lunches, and dinners will you need to pack? How many days of snacks and drink mixes will you need? If you need three breakfasts, put enough oatmeal, cereal, or nutrition bars for three breakfasts into a bag. Do the same for lunch and dinner. It is important to include every item that goes with your staples. For example, what are you going to put on your pasta or rice to make it edible? Are you going to have the same dinner every night or do you want a little variety? Once you assemble your rations, it is a good idea to assemble an extra day's worth of food for emergencies. If you get hung up on the trail, if you underestimate your appetite, or if some food gets eaten by animals, it's comforting to know that you have a little extra. Keep your emergency food stash separate from your other food and tap into it only if you need to.

> "The things you crave on the trail will surprise you. After a few days I usually think about milk and bread and fruit constantly. Once I found a general store and was willing to pay $6 for a pint of ice cream—I didn't even care what flavor!"
>
> —Patty Mills, age 36

Weight and packability

In addition to nutrition and energy content, you also need to consider how much each item of food weighs and how easy it is to pack.

Canned foods and sodas are heavy and bulky—leave them at home. Items like crackers and pastries may be lightweight, but they are difficult to keep from getting crushed. You may not mind eating a bagful of cracker crumbs or a muffin smeared all over its wrapper, but it will surely make a mess. A large bag of puffed rice may occupy too much space in your pack for the number of calories it provides. On the flip side, dense foods such as chocolate and cheese take little space while providing plenty of calories, but if they became the mainstays of your diet, you would probably feel terrible because you wouldn't be getting the right combination of nutrients. The goal is to find foods that are dense, light, compact, and good for you. Energy bars, muesli, beans, and margarine pack a lot of calories into a relatively small serving.

You also want to take foods that won't spoil. Sticking with dehydrated foods is a safe way to go. On shorter trips when you eat your food in a day or two, you can be lenient and carry fresh fruit, vegetables, lunch meat, and bread. But you must do without these luxuries on longer trips.

Food preparation and packaging

The best way I've found to pack lightweight, high-calorie, inexpensive, nutritious foods is to buy the food in bulk and then dehydrate it myself.

A *dehydrator* is a simple apparatus, available at appliance and department stores, that blows warm air onto food and dries it out. After a few hours or a couple days (depending on the food item and your dehydrator), you will have food that contains the same amount of calories and nutrients as it did in its hydrated form, but now lacks the weight of water. Dehydrated foods weigh a fraction of their original weight, won't spoil, and are easy to rehydrate: Just add water and let the food come back to its original form.

Food dehydrator. Food that's been dehydrated retains all its nutrients and calories, but weighs much less.

Our dehydrator has solid plastic trays that fit over the standard porous trays. This way, we can dehydrate liquid foods like soups, stews, and yogurt. The best tasting meals we've ever had on the trail have been homemade concoctions that we dehydrated. Mix up a big batch of your favorite meal, then get rid of the water. My favorite dehydrated meals are spicy black bean soup, stew, hearty ham and bean soup, vegetable stir-fry with red curry, and a white clam sauce to put over pasta. I don't have to worry about preparing a lengthy meal on the trail; I just add water and have a home-cooked meal.

Meat usually doesn't rehydrate as well as sauces and vegetables. Chicken, turkey, beef, and ham take a long time. Rehydrated meat is edible but a little tough to chew. I am not a big meat eater, so I don't mind leaving it out. If you can't stand the thought of dinner without meat, carry a tin of chicken or ham and add it in once the rest of your meal is rehydrated. You can also make jerky in your dehydrator, which can be a tasty snack on the trail.

Experiment before you go. Some foods may need to soak for a long time before you can eat them. Some foods (such as bananas) taste different from their original, hydrated form. Rehydrated carrots and green beans have very strong flavors—too strong for my taste. Broccoli, cauliflower, peas, tomatoes, and potatoes work well for me, and dried pineapple is always the first to disappear.

If you don't own a dehydrator, you can buy food that is already dehydrated. Scan the aisles of your grocery store and search for foods that require you to add only water and boil. Avoid any items that require extended boiling; boiling for more than 10 minutes can rapidly deplete your supply of fuel. Avoid items that require baking, unless you have a backcountry oven. These ovens can be quite a luxury, but they add weight to your pack and extend the time it takes to prepare a meal. Many soup, bean, and pasta dishes are available in dehydrated form, as are hummus, tabouli, and couscous. Dried apricots, apples, raisins, mushrooms, onions, and garlic are common. Turkey and beef jerky can be found in a variety of flavors—from barbecue to teriyaki.

You can also make your own non-dehydrated food. Here are my favorite recipes for granola, trail mix, and energy bars.

GRANOLA

2 cups regular rolled oats
½ cup flaked coconut
½ cup sliced almonds
½ cup shelled sunflower seeds

¼ cup sesame seeds
¾ cup honey
1 tablespoon cooking oil

Combine all ingredients except honey and oil. Mix honey and oil separately then stir into the oat mixture. Put the mixture in a greased pan and bake for 30 minutes at 300 degrees. Stir occasionally.

TRAIL MIX

Mix together any of the following: peanuts, cashews, almonds, pumpkin seeds, sesame sticks, sunflower seeds, pine nuts, coconut shavings, pretzels, cereal (such as Cheerios or Chex), granola, wheat germ, chocolate chips, carob morsels, butterscotch morsels, raisins and other dehydrated fruits such as apricots, pineapples, apples, dates, pears, bananas, cherries, and cranberries.

ENERGY BARS

½ cup peanut butter
½ cup powdered milk
⅓ cup honey

1 envelope unflavored gelatin
1 tablespoon wheat germ

Stir all ingredients, roll into logs, and wrap in foil.

(This recipe is from Harriet Barker's *The One-Burner Gourmet*.)

To cut down on bulky boxes and bags, repackage your food before hitting the trail. Boxes are too bulky and melt in water, and most plastic packaging is not durable or resealable. Take mixes and cereals out of their boxes; remove pasta from its bag. Put rations of spices and sugar in tiny plastic bags or film canisters.

All food needs to be in a waterproof, resealable bag. Keep all food in Ziploc freezer bags or in plastic bags tied in a knot at the top. Then place all your plastic food bags into one stuff sack. I like to use a waterproof stuff sack in case I need to hang my food up on a rainy night.

Some hikers prefer to divide their food for each day and put it in its own bag. I carry my food together, eat what I crave at the moment, and rely on my estimating abilities to have brought the right amounts.

Menu Suggestions

There's a surprising variety of food that works well on the trail. Hot breakfast ideas include oatmeal, instant cream of wheat, and instant grits. I prefer dry cereal or toaster pastries for breakfast, so I don't have to fuss with dishes in the morning or break out the stove. But if it's a chilly morning, a hot breakfast, or at least a hot drink, is worth the effort. I always begin cold mornings with a cup of hot herbal tea.

For me, lunch begins immediately after breakfast and lasts until dinner. It is better for your body to eat many small snacks all day than to stuff yourself with a single, large lunch. Unless it's cold out and you want hot food, you may be better off eating food like cheese and crackers, energy bars, trail mix, bread and peanut butter, dried fruit, and jerky. If you do want to stop and prepare a lunchtime meal, try pasta salad mixes, Lipton Pasta and Sauce packets, and soup mixes. The old standby macaroni and cheese and the inexpensive Ramen noodle packets will get you by, but they may not be the best choices. Mac and cheese has little nutritional value (and personally, I avoid eating anything that is iridescent orange). Ramen noodles are so salty you will want to gulp down jugs of water for hours.

Dinner should be a meal to look forward to. This is the time to break out your homemade, dehydrated concoctions. Other dinner suggestions include: Lipton Pasta and Sauce packets, which can be supplemented with a handful of regular pasta if you want a larger portion; instant mashed potatoes with gravy; dehydrated vegetables and a tin of chicken; pasta with dehydrated tomato sauce or white sauce; rice, vegetables, and curry spices; and instant refried beans with tomatoes and pita bread. While you are waiting for your dinner to cook, you may want to snack on trail mix, or hummus and pita, or make a Lipton Cup-a-Soup to start rehydrating your body. I often catch a chill when I stop moving and settle in for the evening, even on warm days. I make hot chocolate first and munch on animal crackers while dinner is cooking. I usually save a piece of chocolate for dessert.

There are a number of backcountry cookbooks to help you plan your menu. See the "Fuel up" section in the Resource Directory, page 137 for a list.

Sample menus

Below are some sample menus, one for a shorter weekend trip and one for a weeklong trip.

Three days, two nights

Breakfasts (2)

3 cups muesli   1 cup dehydrated milk

Lunches (3)

quarter-pound of cheese   3 energy bars
10 ounces wheat crackers   3 granola bars
small loaf of bread   2 cups mixed dried fruit
1 cup peanut butter

Dinners (2)

1 ½ cups spicy black bean and vegetable soup (rehydrates to about 3 cups)
1 Lipton Pasta and Sauce packet (two servings, but you will eat it as one)
½ cup dehydrated vegetables (mushrooms, onions, peas, corn) to mix into pasta
bag of turkey jerky
1 chocolate bar

Seven days, six nights

Breakfasts (6)

3 cups oatmeal, with 1 cup dried fruit and 2 tablespoons brown sugar
3 cups granola, with 1 cup powdered milk
4 toaster pastries
6 tea bags or coffee packets

Lunches (7)

7 energy bars   2 soup mix packets
7 cups trail mix   2 flavored pasta packets
half-pound of cheese   candy
loaf of bread   2 cups Gatorade mix
1 cup peanut butter

Dinners (6)

handful of jerky   2 chocolate bars
3 cups dehydrated potato stew   3 cups animal crackers
3 cups dehydrated bean soup   1½ cups hot chocolate mix
4 cups macaroni noodles   ½ cup dehydrated sauce

Safe storage in the woods

I spent the first night of my Appalachian Trail hike in the unwelcome company of a dozen mice. All night they tore around the shelter, ran over sleeping bags, and tried to get to suspended food. Their acrobatics were outstanding! During the middle of the night a mouse jumped two feet out from the wall and landed on my hanging food bag. I awoke to bits of trail mix sprinkling on my head.

Animals will do anything to get to your food or to get into a place that smells like food or human scents. Take wildlife seriously. If there are no bears in the area, I like to sleep with my food in the tent. If I am in a shelter, however, I always hang my food and toiletries.

Mice can scale walls and climb down the rope that leads to your hanging food bag. Put in their path an obstacle they can't get around; a tin can or plastic lid usually works. Cut a small hole in the bottom of an empty can or in a plastic coffee-can lid and thread string or rope through the hole. Tie a knot in the string so the can or lid rests on the knot. Attach your food bag to a stick on the bottom of the string. Most mice cannot get around the lid or can. You should also leave zippers and pockets on your backpack open so the critters can explore without chewing holes through your pack.

Some animals—among them, skunks and porcupines—crave salt. I have heard stories about hikers who awoke to find their boots eaten down to the soles. Hang your pack, boots, clothes, and anything else that is sweaty.

The best defense against hungry bears is to use a bearproof canister. These metal canisters weigh about five pounds and have locking lids. Though they appear small, I have been able to fit six days' food in one. Some National Parks sell or rent them to backpackers. Some campsites provide bear boxes. But if the campsite is crowded, there may not be enough room in the bear box for everyone's food.

The third and least reliable method of keeping bears from your food is to hang it by balancing bags over a tree limb. Divide your food into two balanced bags. Toss a rope over a branch that is approximately 20 feet off the ground. The rope should be at least 10 feet from the trunk and on part of a branch that is sturdy

FOOD TIPS

1. Eat the heaviest items and the food that may spoil first.
2. Stop to eat before you get really hungry.
3. Carry crackers, bread, and other crushables in a tennis ball container or a clean milk carton to prevent them from getting crushed.
4. Keep snacks such as energy bars easily accessible.

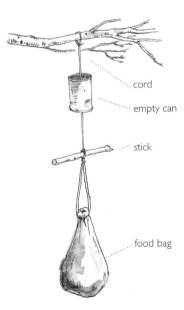

cord

empty can

stick

food bag

To protect your food from mice, use an obstacle like an empty tin can. Hang your food bag on the stick.

Use the counter-balancing method as a last resort to keep food safe from bears. **1:** Choose a limb that cannot support the weight of a bear cub (70 pounds). Tie a food bag to one end of the rope and hoist it up to the branch. **2:** Tie the second bag high on the rope. Tie a loop with the extra rope; you'll use this loop and a long stick to retrieve your bags. **3:** Push the lower bag up with a stick until the bags are at equal height.

enough to support your food—but not the weight of a bear cub. Tie one food bag onto one end of the rope and hoist it to the top. Tie your other food bag as high on the rope as you can; then tie the excess rope in a loop and stuff it in the bag. Use a stick to push the lower bag up so the bags are hanging at the same height. Retrieve your food by sticking the long stick through the loop and pulling your bag down.

WATER

One reason I enjoy backpacking so much is because it makes you pay attention to things that you normally take for granted. Water is a prime example. It is up to you to locate a water source, whether that involves reading a trail guide or studying the contours of the land. You can no longer rely on faucets and running water.

Water is critical during every part of your journey. It is essential for preparing most of your food, which makes a water source a prerequisite for a campsite or resting spot. You need water for washing and cleaning dishes, and, most importantly, for drinking. When you are backpacking in warm or hot weather, you need to consume incredible amounts of water. Experts suggest that your body needs one cup of water for every 20 minutes of rigorous physical exercise. That's a lot of water if you backpack all day. My rule of thumb is to drink as much water as I comfortably can.

Sources

Plan every day around water. From your current destination on the trail, choose a destination for the night that is near water. The easiest way to locate a water source is by looking on your map for a lake, pond, river, stream, wetland, or natural spring close to the trail. Guide books often mention if the water source in a particular area is reliable or if it is known to periodically dry out. Hikers traveling in the opposite direction can also inform you about the availability of water. If you do find yourself in a predicament and desperately need water, think about where water would most likely collect. Water naturally drains off slopes, so your first thought should be to head down into a valley. Then look for dense vegetation.

If water is abundant, I don't carry more than a quart while hiking. I make a point to stop frequently at water sources and drink. (It is highly advisable to purify found water before you drink it. Treatment techniques are discussed on pages 80–83.) If there is any doubt about the availability of water, carry extra with you. I like to carry two 1-quart Lexan water bottles with screw-on lids

"The guidebook said there was a creek two miles ahead, so I bypassed the pond. I walked for more than an hour and never found it. It must have dried up. I had no water left and no reliable water source to head for, so I turned around, bit my lip, and headed back to the pond. Those were the longest, most frustrating two miles of my backpacking career."

—Mandy Williams, age 34

so I know they won't leak. Lexan is a material that is virtually unbreakable, doesn't allow bacteria to grow on it, and doesn't absorb the odor of the liquids you put in it. Be wary of cheap plastic bottles; they will eventually crack. Also, avoid cyclists' water bottles with the pull-up spout; they almost always leak.

If you are traveling in an arid climate or over a stretch of land that is particularly dry, you may need to carry enough water to drink for the entire day and to cook that night. A water bag, or bladder bag, is an efficient, compact, lightweight way to carry a lot of water. Believe it or not, for something as simple as a water bag, there are still a variety of styles, materials, and volumes to choose from. New pack designs often come with a water bag built into the pack. A hose that runs from the bag can be clipped on to your shoulder strap so you can easily access water while you walk. Most water bags will do the job, so it is really a matter of preference.

Lexan water bottle

Bladder bag

Carrying some type of water bag is necessary in any environment. You will use it to transport water from the source to your campsite. The nearest water source may be a half-mile from your camp. After a day of backpacking, you won't want to make more than one trip to get water. If you have a 4-quart bladder bag plus two 1-quart jugs, you will have plenty of water to drink during the evening, cook dinner and breakfast, clean dishes, brush your teeth, and carry the next morning until you reach another source.

Treatment

Thirty years ago, hikers drank from most mountain streams without worrying about getting sick. But today virtually all of our water sources are contaminated. Even a clear mountain stream or a bubbling spring can contain nasty viruses, bacteria, organic chemicals, and parasitic protozoa like the well-known *Giardia lamblia*.

The symptoms of *Giardia* appear a couple weeks after ingestion. They include diarrhea, nausea, stomachache, and a bloated feeling. If you think you have contracted *Giardia*, consult a physician. *Giardia* can be treated with antibiotics. I once met a hiker who drank from any stream he pleased, and he never treated the water. Instead he carried the antibiotics to fight *Giardia* should he contract it. This is one strategy that I don't recommend.

It's important to understand that you can get sick not only from drinking contaminated water but also from using dirty cookware and utensils, washing your body with stream water and then handling food, and not washing your hands after going to the bathroom.

Some sources suggest that there has been too much hype about *Giardia* and that the odds of actually becoming infected are about the same as getting attacked by a shark. The media may have given the little protozoan more credit than it deserves. However, I have known or heard of many people who have contracted *Giardia*, and I've never met a soul who has been attacked by a shark.

Many people drink untreated water in the wilderness and have never gotten sick. It's a gamble. The practice could save you the time and energy of treating water (not to mention the weight of a water treatment device) or it could leave you in bed for weeks with severe diarrhea. This is one gamble I'm not willing to take. There are three ways to treat water: boiling, chemical treatments, and filtration.

Boiling

Boiling water is the most effective treatment. Bringing water to a rolling boil is enough to kill all the microorganisms, and there is no need to boil it for a certain length of time. This is an easy way to treat water at camp, since you need to boil water anyway for your meal. Of course, boiling water in the middle of a hike is inconvenient, because it takes a lot of time and fuel. Also, what if your stove breaks or you run out of fuel? I like to use boiling as a backup method and depend on chemical treatments as my primary method.

Chemical treatment

Iodine and chlorine tablets, crystals, or concentrated liquid can be used to treat drinking water. The tablets are lightweight and easy to use, although you may have to wait 20 minutes or so before you can safely drink the water. Some people don't like the taste of the chemically treated water. It has been my experience that if you're thirsty enough, you'll drink almost anything.

One alternative to tablets is iodine crystals. The Polar-Pur Iodine Crystal Kit can treat 2,000 quarts of water. I used this kit for half of my Appalachian Trail hike and was very pleased. Water treated with crystals seems to taste better than water treated with tablets.

One note of caution when using chemical treatments: *Backpacker* magazine reports that iodine does not kill the protozoan *Cryptosporidium*, which is becoming more common in North American waters. This protozoan is similar to *Giardia*, but it seems that most hikers, including myself, are willing to take this risk. However, if you are concerned about *Cryptosporidium*, you may want to treat your water with one of the other methods. Iodine may also be harmful if you are pregnant or nursing or have thyroid problems or goiters. If you have any of these conditions, you may want to steer away from iodine treatments and use one of the other methods.

If you like the idea of chemical treatment because it is inexpensive, lightweight, and easy to do, but you are not thrilled about the iodine aftertaste, add some flavor to the water. Drink mixes such as Crystal Light, Kool-Aid, and Tang add zest to your drink. These powdered mixes can also give you an excellent energy boost and provide you with more calories during the hike. Gatorade and other electrolyte-containing thirst quenchers are good choices.

Filters

One night my partner and I arrived at a campsite in the dark. We were exhausted, so we ate a cold dinner and fetched some water from the shallow creek for the night. We treated the water with iodine tablets and settled into our sleeping bags. A couple times during the night I woke up thirsty and took a few gulps. We rose with the light of the new day and fired up the stove for breakfast. When I poured water into the pot for tea, we saw that it was dirt-brown with chunks of leaves and debris. I had been drinking it all night and never knew! Boiling and iodine tablets will kill microorganisms, but these methods don't filter out noticeable particles. Only a water filter can separate visible particles, such as bits of leaves and bugs, from the water.

Water filters (1) and **purifiers (2)** are popular devices for treating water.

With a filter, you can drink immediately: You don't have to wait for boiled water to cool or clutch your jug in one hand and your watch in the other while you wait for the iodine tablets to do their job. Compared to chemical treatments, filtration is a heavy and expensive method. (Filters range from $30 to $300.) Additionally, if you are traveling in cold conditions, the water in your filter may freeze and render it useless.

Water filters are very popular and there are a number of different kinds to choose from. Filters remove bacteria, organic chemicals, and protozoa like *Giardia* and *Cryptosporidium*. Most filters don't remove viruses—the tiniest and most dangerous microorganisms. Few people worry about viruses in North America. However, they are becoming increasingly more prevalent in our waters. If you travel abroad, especially to Third World countries, be sure to use a filter that removes viruses or use an alternative treatment method like boiling or iodine.

If you decide to buy a water filter, consider if you want a regular filter or a more expensive *purifier* that also gets rid of viruses. Consider how many quarts of water it will filter before the actual filter needs to be cleaned or replaced. Filters need to be cleaned or replaced often. To make your filter last longer, avoid filtering visibly dirty water. Use a coffee filter as a prefilter: Put it over the intake hose to prevent debris from clogging the filter. As you are filtering, keep the intake hose from resting on the bottom of the stream, and keep your input and output hoses away from each other to avoid contaminating the clean output hose. When you do clean the filter, keep the contaminated filter away from the output hose and other kitchenware to avoid spreading harmful pathogens. You may want to flush your filter with bleach to prevent microorganisms from multiplying on your filter while it's being stored for long periods of time. To do so, put a capful of bleach in a quart jug and filter the water. Make sure all the water is out of the tubes before you stow it away.

If you run out of iodine tablets, or your filter clogs, or your stove breaks, it is important to keep drinking water. Dehydration can be a far more serious condition than a case of the runs.

If you must drink untreated water, here are a few suggestions. If you see signs of animals (beaver dam, livestock, a mouse carcass, deer scat), go upstream. Most bacteria and protozoa are transferred via animals. Look for steep snowy slopes: There is less of a chance that animals have contaminated such areas. Look for natural springs. There is no guarantee that a spring is clean, but it will most likely be better than drinking from a large, muddy river. As a general rule, steer clear of water near agricultural areas, logging or mining operations, and heavy industry.

KITCHENWARE

Stoves

Gone are the days of building fires to cook your meals. People now realize that campfires strip wilderness areas of important dead wood that would naturally be recycled into the soil to provide nutrients for other growth. Fire rings and burnt rocks scar the land, and a small campfire can easily get out of hand under the wrong conditions. (It is hard to beat the romance and warming power of a campfire, though; if you feel you must have one, follow the important guidelines outlined in Chapter 9, page 120.)

Stoves are the preferred method for cooking. They don't remove or damage nature. They are also a much easier way to generate heat—especially if it's cold or wet out. Providing hot food and drink to the weary backpacker, a stove can be your most treasured possession. However, if it's on the fritz or if you don't know how to use it, it can be rather intimidating. A stove is a valuable asset to any backpacking trip, but it is up to you to make sure that it works and that you know how to use it.

When you buy a stove, ask yourself the following questions. Do you need a three-season stove or one that works in the winter as well? What kind of fuel do you prefer: butane or propane canisters, auto gas, kerosene, alcohol, or white gas? Also consider how quickly a stove can bring water to a boil and how much it weighs. This sounds more complicated than it truly is: Selecting a stove is not that difficult since there aren't that many models to choose from. There are two basic types of stoves: those that burn liquid fuel and those that burn butane/propane canisters.

Some stoves that burn liquid fuels will burn *any* of the liquid fuels: white gas, kerosene, alcohol, auto gas. The preferred fuel for most liquid fuel stoves is white gas, which is most often

WATER TIPS

1. Make sure the water bottle's lid attaches to the bottle so you don't lose it.

2. Use a bandanna to filter out large particles in your water if you are treating it by boiling or by using iodine.

3. Keep the threads on your water bottle and lid clean, or bacteria and mold will take over.

4. Slip a wool sock around your water bottle to keep it warmer in the winter and cooler in the summer.

5. On freezing nights, store full water bottles upside down so water won't freeze in the threads and make your bottle impossible to open. On severely frozen nights, sleep with your jug in your sleeping bag.

STOVE TIPS

• • • • • • • • • • • • • • • • • • •

1. I recommend using a mini-lighter instead of matches to light your stove. But bring a few matches in a waterproof container as a backup.

2. In cold temperatures or windy conditions, it will take longer for your stove to boil water. Windscreens are helpful to shield your stove and trap the heat.

3. The amount of fuel to bring depends on how many meals you cook, how long you cook per meal, the intensity of the flame you cook over, and the weather.

4. Keep your head and body away from the flame, especially when you're lighting your stove.

5. Synthetic materials, such as many backpacking clothes and your tent, are highly flammable.

continued on page 85

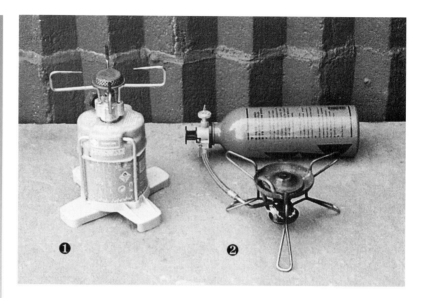

1. Propane/butane canister stove and 2. Liquid fuel stove.

referred to as Coleman fuel. White gas is inexpensive and is sold at outfitting and hardware stores as well as some supermarkets. Kerosene is also inexpensive and readily available, but it's more difficult to light. Stoves that run on denatured alcohol are the most environmentally friendly, although the fuel is often expensive and hard to come by. Auto gas should be used as a last resort since it has a tendency to clog fuel lines and to leave a residue of black soot on the stove and your pots.

Many hikers prefer stoves that use propane/butane canisters because they're lightweight and easy to use. I don't use canisters because they have to be thrown out and replaced. Some companies, however, are beginning to recycle the canisters. Keep in mind that on longer hikes where you need to resupply in towns, the right canister may be hard to find. And they cannot be sent in the mail. Primus now makes a stove called the Multi-Fuel System; it can use either liquid fuels or canisters, depending on your preference and on what's readily available.

The MSR Whisperlite Internationale is one of the most popular and well-reviewed stoves on the market because it is self cleaning, lightweight, powerful, and dependable. It burns white gas, which is usually easy to find. It was by far the most used stove on the Appalachian Trail and has served me well for years.

Before you buy a stove, have a salesperson demonstrate how to light it. Then do it yourself. I bought my stove without asking to be shown how to light it. I remember sitting out on my porch,

Lighting a stove is easier than you think!

STOVE TIPS

(continued from page 84)

6. Some major airlines permit you to transport properly purged stoves and fuel bottles, while others don't. A stove and fuel bottle can be purged by emptying the fuel and exposing them to air and sunlight for a few hours. Find out before you get to the airport if your stove can come with you or not. You may have to ship it ahead of time or buy one when you get to your destination.

7. If your stove is not self cleaning, it probably came with a stove-pricker, which you'll use to clean the jet should it get clogged during your trip.

8. Paint the outside of your pot with black, heat-resistant paint to decrease the boiling time.

9. Water boils faster when you cover the pot with a lid.

reading every step of the lighting procedure very carefully, and feeling terrified that I was going to do something wrong and blow it up. I attached the fuel bottle to the stove, pumped it to build pressure, tentatively allowed some fuel to prime the wick, closed the fuel valve, and lit the liquid fuel. But I was too eager to turn it on. As I opened the fuel valve, flames shot three feet into the air. The next time, I lit the liquid fuel to prime it and waited much longer—until the flame was almost out and it was fully primed. Then I opened the fuel valve. That time, I heard the hiss of vapors and a blue flame danced on the burner. So it wasn't that hard after all!

When you get your stove home, light it a couple times. You will soon master the art of lighting it and wonder why you ever thought it would be a hard thing to do.

Make sure to thoroughly read and understand your stove's manual. Know what type of fuel it can use and what type it can't, know how to light it, how often to clean it (which involves unclogging the fuel line and jet, unless you have a self-cleaning stove), and how to store it. After a couple trips you will become comfortable with your stove, develop the "right touch" to get it to simmer and boil, and be able to estimate how much fuel you burn each day.

Cookware

Cookware should be kept to a minimum. I carry a 2-quart stainless steel pot and lid, a plastic cup, and a Lexan plastic spoon. This combination works well if I am alone or with one other person.

The lid can serve as a plate or bowl and one person can eat out of the pot. If you are traveling in a group, you may want to bring one large pot and a lightweight plastic bowl for each person. There

is no need to bring a lot of pots unless you are determined to prepare a multicourse meal. There is also no need to bring a knife and fork; there is nothing that a spoon can't scoop up (although spaghetti can be a challenge). A small (clean!) pocket knife is the only blade you'll need.

Aluminum cookware is the lightest and least expensive but is difficult to clean and not very durable. Stainless steel is heavier but extremely durable and easy to clean. The new titanium cookware is light and durable, but it's expensive.

Cookware: pot, lid, cup, spoon, pot grab

Another excellent (but expensive) choice is the aluminum/ stainless steel combination. It is durable, lightweight, and boils water faster than the stainless steel pots.

Some people bring multiple pots and frying pans and lots of utensils. The latest accessory in the well-equipped camp kitchen is the oven. The Bakepacker and the Outback Oven, available from outdoor gear suppliers, are designed to convert your camp stove into an oven, so you can prepare once-unheard-of trail foods like pizza, biscuits, and cakes. I feel I can survive for a couple days without baked food, and I wouldn't want to carry the extra weight on an extended trip. I just hope that no one I encounter on the trail will have one: There's nothing worse than watching someone prepare a pizza or bake fresh bread while you sit there and stir up another dehydrated dinner!

Washing dishes

It is as important to properly clean your cookware as it is to treat your water. Plus, it is important to do this in an environmentally friendly way. First, try to prepare an appropriate portion of food so you won't have to deal with leftovers. If you do make too much food, store leftovers in a plastic bag or water jug or add them to your trash and pack them out. Never bury food or dump leftovers in a stream.

Likewise, you should never wash your pots in a water source and let food and soap drift downstream. Gravel and sand are good for scouring your pots. If you use soap, use a biodegradable soap (available at outfitters). Scrub out the pot with a small scrubbing pad and soap; then scatter the waste on the ground at least 150 feet from the water source. If you are in bear country, dig a hole six inches deep, pour your waste water in the hole, and cover it up. To prevent contaminating your cookware with untreated water, use only treated water to wash dishes and utensils. You should sterilize your pots and utensils with boiling water at least every few days.

Chapter 7

SAFETY AND COMFORT

SAFETY

When you go backpacking, you rely on yourself not only to carry everything you need to survive, but also to use your equipment and your common sense to avoid situations that could jeopardize your safety. As an informed backpacker, you should be aware of a number of risks associated with backcountry travel and know what to do if you find yourself in a threatening situation. Injuries, blisters, heat exhaustion, hypothermia, animals, hunters, and people all pose potential threats to your safety. However, as a cautious and informed backpacker you will greatly reduce your risk of getting hurt. And keep in mind that there are far more threats to your health in civilization than there are in the wilderness.

"**E**ven after spending many nights alone, rumors and real-life events still cause a fear to reside in me. It could also be good, common-sense caution!"

—Sara Hurley, age 24

First-aid

The bulk of your backpacking battle wounds will undoubtedly be minor cuts, scrapes, and blisters. These can all be patched and protected with the contents of a good first-aid kit. The following items are essential to pack into the woods:

- Band-Aids
- Neosporin or another antibiotic ointment
- sterile gauze pads
- adhesive tape or duct tape
- 10cc irrigation syringe with an 18-gauge catheter tip for flushing out cuts
- latex surgical gloves
- moleskin or your choice of blister coverings
- nonaspirin pain reliever
- elastic bandage to wrap a hurt ankle, knee, elbow, or wrist
- needle for splinters or blisters
- matches to sterilize needle
- first-aid book

The amount of each item you pack will depend on the length of the trip and how injury prone you think you are. Halfway through my Appalachian Trail hike, my first-aid kit was reduced to Neosporin, Advil, and a tiny roll of duct tape for blisters. That was risky. If I sprained my ankle or had a serious cut, I would have been in trouble. Don't skimp on first-aid. Make sure the contents in your kit haven't expired. Put the contents of your kit in a double Ziploc bag and keep it in a place that is easy to access. I like to keep my first-aid supplies in the top pouch of my pack.

To become more confident about your ability to take care of yourself and treat others in the wilderness, you may want to enroll in a first-aid course or read more about wilderness medicine. Community groups, the Red Cross, outdoor outfitters, Outward Bound, National Outdoor Leadership School, and some clubs may offer classes or be able to steer you in the right direction. Organizations like SOLO, Wilderness Medicine Institute, Wilderness Medical Associates, and the National Association for Search and Rescue offer Wilderness First Responder and Wilderness Emergency Medical Technician certification. There also are numerous books devoted to the subject of first-aid in the wilderness, many of which are listed in the "Go safely" section of the Resource Directory, page 139.

Common injuries

Backpacking injuries usually occur when you get fatigued. You are more prone to slip or trip after a few hours of strenuous travel. When your body begins to get tired, your concentration may wane and you may not have the energy to lift your feet as high as you should. Injuries due to fatigue are frustrating, because you know that if you had allowed yourself to rest you might not have gotten hurt. So rest often!

When you feel yourself wearing down, evaluate your present condition. If you decide to push on, concentrate on every step. Be careful not to rely on a slippery rock or a rotting log for support. Place each foot with purpose and don't step blindly and carelessly. If the terrain is challenging and technical, you may want to call it a day and tackle the rough stuff after a good night's sleep.

If you or someone in your group does get injured, you should be prepared to give the victim basic first-aid treatment. Even if you have never had first-aid training, you probably know how to treat backpacking's most common injuries—cuts, twisted ankles, and blisters.

Cuts

To treat a cut, stop the bleeding, clean the cut, apply antibiotic ointment to prevent infection, and cover it with a Band-Aid or with gauze and adhesive tape. When stopping the bleeding, apply pressure and don't remove the sterile gauze pad or cloth until the bleeding has stopped. When you are in contact with another person's blood, it is a good idea to wear latex gloves. The most important part about treating a cut is knowing how to clean it. Use a syringe and catheter tip to squirt water into the cut to flush out dirt and bacteria. Only use treated water (water treatment methods are discussed in Chapter 6). If you don't have a syringe, prick a pin-sized hole in a plastic bag, close the top, and squirt water through the hole. This method is not as effective as using a syringe, but it's better than nothing.

Twisted ankles

Treat a twisted ankle by soaking it in cold water (such as a stream), elevating the foot, and taping the ankle or wrapping it with an Ace bandage. Give the victim a pain reliever. Next determine if she can continue the next day or if someone needs to go for help. If the ankle is swollen or she is limping without carrying her pack, encourage her to stay off her feet.

Blisters

Beginners and advanced backpackers alike experience blisters. Your feet will eventually toughen to the occasion, but here are some preventive measures.

Make sure your boots fit properly and they are broken in before your trip. Wear a thin, non-cotton liner sock to help reduce the friction from a rubbing boot, and apply foot powder a couple times a day to keep your feet dryer and less prone to blisters. The best thing you can do is take care of sore spots before they develop into blisters. If you feel a hot spot (a place that burns), you should stop hiking and put a protective layer on that area. Band-Aids generally slide off during the course of the day; many hikers prefer moleskin, which is cotton flannel with adhesive on the back. Others swear by Spenco's Second Skin. If you are like me and have very sweaty feet, everything you try may slide off the sore spot and ball up in your sock. I now use duct tape exclusively.

If a true blister forms, clean the bubble, pop it with a sterile needle or knife tip, and drain out the fluid. Leave the top layer of skin intact to serve as a protective layer. Apply antibiotic ointment and cover the blister. It is best to periodically remove the bandage and clean the blister to prevent it from becoming infected. That is the drawback of using duct tape: You may be stuck with it for days since you will certainly not want to peel off anything that is securely fastened to a tender blister. To avoid this, place a small piece of gauze over the blister before covering it with duct tape. If it is too painful to walk, reduce your mileage or take a day off. For more serious injuries such as stress fractures or serious burns, refer to the first-aid book in your kit.

Bugs

If you are traveling anywhere that has even a remote chance of being infested with biting insects, add bug repellent and anti-itch ointment to your first-aid kit. I guarantee that these two items may become your most treasured possessions. Whether your choice of bug dope is all-natural citronella, Skin So Soft, or 100-percent DEET, you will be thankful you have it. Still, I am not convinced that any of these repellents actually prevent *all* mosquitoes from attacking. Even 100-percent DEET failed me in the marshlands of Massachusetts, and the smallest amount made me flushed and dizzy.

There has been a good deal of controversy over the use of DEET. Many people swear it's the only stuff that works, and they claim that it's perfectly safe if used in small amounts and in concentrations less than 50 percent.

Nevertheless, you do need to be concerned about a few things if you decide to use DEET on a backpacking trip. First, never put DEET on children. They are too small and DEET is too toxic. Second, keep it away from your face, and be careful to get as little as possible on your hands to avoid accidentally wiping your eyes with DEET-soaked fingers. Third, don't put DEET under your clothes where you don't need it anyway. If you apply it to your clothes, keep in mind that DEET can eat through plastics and synthetic materials—like the ones used for most backpacking clothes. Fourth, DEET of any concentration should be washed off at the end of the day. This presents a problem in the backcountry. Avoid washing DEET off in a stream; if it eats through plastic and is toxic to children, imagine what it will do to fish and the other critters in the stream.

There are some natural, commonsense defenses you can employ. First, mosquitoes don't like strong wind and sun. If you stop for lunch on a windy ridge in the heat of the day, you may actually get to enjoy that peanut butter sandwich after all. Second, fragrant humans and bright colors attract mosquitoes. We are fragrant from soap, laundry detergents, shampoo, hair spray, moisturizing lotion, deodorant, etc. There *are* advantages to being dirty. Hang your clothes in the wind to rid them of detergent residue, and leave anything fragrant at home. Wearing earth tones will help too. Third, rapid movements like swatting, slapping, and shooing attract more mosquitoes. Remain calm.

The smoke from a small fire will deter the critters, but the most effective refuge in mosquito territory is a tent and long sleeves and pants when you are outside the tent. A mesh head net that covers my head, face, and neck was one of the best investments I ever made. When I'm outside the tent, I can be certain that at least my head and neck will be bug free.

HYPERTHERMIA

Late one November a couple years ago, I inadvertently tortured my dog. I never would have brought my Alaskan malamute to the desert if I had known it would be so hot. But it was a cool morning in Moab, Utah, so I headed out for a mountain bike ride. Few things please Kodiak more than chasing bikes. But after an hour or so, the temperature soared and Kodiak was resting under every shrub and scrub he could find. By that point we were seven miles into our route and had no choice but to keep going. He dug holes to uncover deeper, cooler earth and lay down in them. He asked me for water constantly. With a fur coat designed for subzero temperatures, Kodiak was in a tough predicament. I stopped frequently, was careful not to push him, and gave him quarts of water. His instincts to keep cool were right on, and he managed to complete the thirteen-mile trail.

If you backpack in the summer or in desert environments, you may find yourself in a similar situation. You risk suffering from hyperthermia, an illness that occurs when your body overheats. You need to be able to recognize when the heat is too much and how to treat hyperthermic conditions such as heat exhaustion and heat stroke.

Heat exhaustion

Heat exhaustion is caused by the loss of water and salt through sweating. It results in the body's inability to regulate its temperature. A person experiencing heat exhaustion will sweat profusely, have pale and clammy skin and rapid and shallow breathing, and may complain of dizziness, weakness, and a headache. When treating heat exhaustion, move the victim to a cool area and wipe the victim's face and neck with a damp bandanna. Elevate the victim's feet and have her sip water.

Heat stroke

Heat stroke is a more severe condition. A person experiencing heat stroke will have a flushed face and hot, dry skin. The victim may have a strong and rapid pulse and slow and loud breath, and she may become unconscious. Have the victim lie down with her head and shoulders propped up and maintain an open airway. Cover her body and head with wet clothes and fan the victim. Transport the victim to a medical facility as soon as possible. It is extremely difficult for two or three people to carry someone out of the woods. It may be close to impossible over long distances and technical terrain. Unless you are in a group of six or more, it may be better to go for help than to try to move the victim yourself.

Prevention

You can avoid these adverse heat conditions by taking the following precautions.

- Make sure water is readily available and drink often.

- Drink before you get thirsty.

- Salts are rapidly depleted through sweating. Eating salty foods will help your body retain water and replenish lost electrolytes. Dried fruits, chocolate, nuts, and salty seeds will help restore your electrolyte balance.

- Wear appropriate clothing: a thin, long-sleeved, light-colored shirt; sunglasses; a visor.

- Dip a bandanna in a stream every chance you get and use it to cool your face.

- Dunk your head in cool water.

- Rest often in shady spots and don't do anything too strenuous. Conserve your energy.

- Avoid walking in the heat of the day. Hike in the morning and evening and find a cool spot to rest during the day.

- Like Kodiak, if you stop frequently in the shade, drink often, and don't over-exert yourself, you can have an enjoyable trip despite the heat.

HYPOTHERMIA

Hypothermia is a condition whereby the body is chilled and cannot raise its core temperature. This is an interesting condition because you want to warm up, but you are often so delirious that you can't logically figure out how to do it—even if you are sitting beside a pile of wood and matches.

A hypothermic condition can arise in temperatures as high as 50 degrees. A victim may not know she is hypothermic, so it is important to recognize the signs. They include shivering, numbness, low body temperature, muscle weakness, drowsiness, mumbling, and incoherence. Victims often don't know they are in danger. They sometimes want to lie down and go to sleep. If they sleep, they usually die.

Treat a victim by getting her out of the wind and rain, removing her wet clothes, and getting the person into a sleeping bag. You too may want to crawl inside the bag and use your body heat to warm the victim. Build a fire and give the victim hot liquids. Get her to a medical facility as soon as possible.

A hypothermic condition can arise very quickly. You may not feel at all cold when hiking in a cool rain. But as soon as you stop, your body stops producing heat. You may begin to lose crucial motor skills and may not be able to open your pack, unwrap a granola bar, or strike a match. There are a number of precautions you should take to prevent a hypothermic condition:

- Bundle up and fuel up on high-energy foods before you begin to get chilled.

- Don't stay too long on a windy summit during a rainy day or in a cold stream. Your body can cool down faster than you think—especially in wet or windy conditions.

- Always have a dry change of clothes, even if it means getting up in the morning and changing into cold, wet clothes. A set of dry clothes at the end of the day could save your life. Unless you are in danger of suffering from hypothermia when you get up, wet clothes will warm on your body as soon as you start moving (proper backpacking clothing is discussed in Chapter 4).

- If you are cold in the morning when you wake up or at night before bed, do some exercises in your sleeping bag (sit-ups, squeeze your buttocks, press your legs or hands together) and have a hot drink. You have a better chance of staying warm if you don't start out cold.

- Wear a hat and gloves. Most of your body heat is lost through your head, and it is important to keep your fingers warm and nimble.

- Dress in layers of synthetics, fleece, or wool. Cotton kills. If you are wearing cotton and you start to get wet and chilled, it is best to take off the cotton and replace it with a noncotton shirt or just a jacket.

- Don't wear an extra layer of socks. Your toes need to move to stay warm.

- If it looks like it is going to rain, have a snack since you may not want to stop for a snack in the middle of a downpour. Also, if you are resting at a shelter and it looks like it might rain, consider whether it is worth pressing on.

ANIMALS

We normally consider ourselves at the top of the food chain and pay little attention to the risk of being injured or eaten by another animal. But there are a few animals that pose a potential threat to humans. The most common ones are ticks, spiders, snakes, and bears. There are bees and wasps, too, and you probably already know if you're allergic to stings. You also need to be aware of other animals—like scorpions in the desert, and mountain lions in the West—and know what to do if you encounter one on the trail. Contact the National Park Service or U.S.D.A. Forest Service to get information on animals that inhabit the area you will be traveling (see page 143).

Ticks

I included ticks among the four most common threatening animals because they are so abundant. Especially in the east, ticks are prevalent between May and July. Hiking in Virginia in May, I pulled up to 10 ticks a day off my dog.

If you are traveling in tick country, wear light-colored clothes to make ticks easier to spot and search yourself and a partner for ticks a few times a day. Tuck the cuffs of your pants into your socks so they can't crawl up your pants leg. If you do get a tick, pull it out gently by grasping it with tweezers as close to your skin as possible. You can also coat the tick with oil, thereby clogging its airways and forcing it to release its grip. Clean the bite immediately. Every tick bite will not cause you to become sick. Many disease-causing bacteria spread by ticks require that the tick be attached to you for hours or even days to successfully transmit the disease.

The deer tick has received the most attention because, along with the western black-legged tick, it can transmit Lyme disease. Because deer ticks are so small—about the size of the tip of a pencil—they are hard to find. If you get bitten by a deer tick, you may not know it. Their bite can sometimes cause a circular rash with a clear center. But if you experience flulike symptoms such as fatigue, muscle and joint pain, swollen glands, sore throat, and a headache, you should get tested for Lyme disease. Unlike the flu, Lyme disease will not go away with time; its symptoms can, in fact, worsen.

Spiders

There are only three types of spiders in the United States that are officially considered venomous by the Centers for Disease Control and Prevention: the widow spiders, the recluse spiders, and the hobo spider.

Widow spiders are found throughout the United States and southern Canada, especially in the east. The brown recluse is found in the Midwest and parts of the South, while other recluse

EVACUATION

Evacuation from the backcountry is no easy task. Unless you are in a group of at least six people, can construct a stretcher, and are physically able to carry the injured person to civilization, it is better to leave the victim and go for help. If there are more than just the two of you, one person should stay with the victim while the other or others go for help. This is where a map and compass may come in handy; you may have to find a shortcut to a road or town.

Before you go for help, write down the following information. When you're under pressure, these points could slip your mind, so it's a good idea to have them recorded.

- victim's age, health concerns, current medication
- description of the injury (signs and symptoms) and how it happened
- time the injury occurred
- what action has been taken to help the victim
- exact location of victim

spiders are found in the Southwest. The hobo spider resides in the Northwest. Although the media tends to sensationalize spider bites (and many bites from unseen insects are often attributed to spiders), spider bites do occur and can be serious in some cases.

The bites of the hobo and recluse spiders are similar. The bite produces a lesion on your skin and gives you flulike symptoms. The bite of a black widow, a common type of widow spider, may be unnoticeable on your skin but may produce severe cramps, nausea, and sweating.

One other type of spider, called the yellow sac spider, is common and widespread. Its bite produces a lesion, as well as instant stinging pain, redness, swelling, and itching. Although not officially listed as venomous, treat a bite by this spider as you would treat a bite by the venomous spiders.

If you believe you have been bitten, get to a doctor immediately or send someone for help. Don't move the part of your body that was bitten, and keep the bitten limb dangling down. Leave the bite unbandaged to encourage bleeding and rid your body of as much poison as possible; then apply a cold, wet bandanna to the bite. It will be very helpful if you can describe to a physician the spider that bit you.

Contrary to popular belief, spiders do not typically attack people. They only bite if they are provoked, trapped, or defending eggs. The best prevention is to shake out boots and clothing before putting them on your body and to pay attention to where you place your hands on rocks. Also, be careful what you touch in outhouses. Spiders often reside in the corners of backcountry toilets.

Snakes

Why are so many people afraid of snakes? Many scientists believe that our fear was carried over from our ancestors, the apes. Snakes were a major threat to apes. It is believed that the apes who learned to avoid snakes survived, and those survivors evolved into humans. Whether it's evolutionary baggage or not, many of us are afraid and want to know what to do if we encounter a slithering serpent.

Only four groups of snakes in North America are venomous. The rattlesnake is common throughout much of the United States. The cottonmouth, or water moccasin, is found in Southeastern swamps. Copperheads are found in the East. And the coral snake is found in the Southwest and Southeast.

During the evening, snakes may come out from underneath rocks to hunt for rodents, but snakes are not after you—you are far too big. Most snake bites occur when a person steps on a snake or reaches toward a snake (usually inadvertently), making it feel threatened. Watch where you step and where you place your hands as you move along rocky terrain. I always feel more comfortable wearing sturdy boots and gaiters in snake country.

If you do get bitten, there is still a chance that the bite is not poisonous. Roughly half of bites from poisonous snakes actually have venom in them. If you are unlucky and begin to experience a stinging pain around the bite, severe burning, nausea, weakness, rapid pulse or belabored breathing, you need to seek professional help immediately. A good addition to a first-aid kit is the

Sawyer Venom Extractor; use it to suck out venom within one minute of being bitten. (After a minute has elapsed, the extractor will do little good.) Do not cut the victim, use a tourniquet, or apply ice to the wound. The best way to treat a snakebite victim is to treat the person for shock and get her to a medical facility within 12 hours. If it is not possible to move the victim, go for help and bring a professional to the victim.

Bears

Bears no longer occupy many of the regions they once did. However, there are many places across North America where you still can encounter bears. Two types of bears live in our woods: black bears and grizzlies.

Black bears are the most common of the North American bears, and they are found across the continent. Despite the name, black bears may be blonde, honey colored, brown, or black. They are active day or night, but they generally feed in the morning and evening. It is comforting to know that 90 percent of their diet consists of plants and the rest is typically insects and the carcasses of dead animals. You can tell if a bear is near by spotting its tracks or by smelling it; they smell like a combination of wet dog and skunk. Also, keep your eyes and ears open. You may be able to spot a bear or hear it from a distance and be able to back away safely. Black bears are more of a threat to your food and gear than they are to your life.

Black bear tracks. The hind foot measures about 7 inches and looks similar to a human foot. The front foot is considerably shorter. All bears have five toes, but in some tracks only four may show. As bears walk, they place the larger hind foot in front of the front foot.

Anne Thiessen, age 36, learned about bears the hard way. "I was in Kings Canyon, California, for a ten-day trip. Lots of food, great food, was hung a hundred yards away from the tent. It was the first morning of the trip, and we went to take our food down for breakfast. When we got to the tree, all that was left were two tins of chicken and shredded stuff sacs left by one hungry bear. We hadn't heard a thing, but another group of campers relayed the story of the persistent bear who, after climbing near our stash, methodically reached with front, then back, paws to snag the string. Once the bear got the bag down, he ate everything. He even took water breaks to wash down the peanut butter! I have no idea why they didn't chase him away. But they did give us four or five

• •

"**W**e hadn't heard a thing, but another group of campers relayed the story of the persistent bear who, after climbing near our stash, methodically reached with front, then back, paws to snag the string. Once the bear got the bag down, he ate everything. He even took water breaks to wash down the peanut butter!"

—Anne Thiessen, age 36

• •

"**M**y most memorable moment backpacking has to be when we were in bear country and sang Elton John songs as loud as we could while visiting the wilderness equivalent of 'porcelain.' What a music video that would make!"

—Sonya Fellows, age 33

'lean' days of food so we could continue our trip. We were quite creative with our food-hanging techniques the next few nights, including digging a two-foot pit under the hanging bag when the trees became too small to do the job."

If you do encounter a black bear, it will most likely avoid you; however, every situation is different. If you see a bear that hasn't seen you, talk loudly to let the bear discover your presence. Back away slowly while facing the bear and avoid direct eye contact, which a bear may perceive as a threat. Coming between a female and her cubs can be downright dangerous. If you see a cub, move away from it. Never try to outrun or outswim a bear or climb a tree—you will most certainly take second place. If you are attacked by a black bear, fight back. Black bears have been driven away by people who have defended themselves with rocks, sticks, and their bare hands.

Grizzly bears are more aggressive than black bears. Although they used to live in many parts of the country, we have reduced their populations in North America to the Pacific Northwest, western Canada, and Alaska. Grizzlies are so abundant in parts of Alaska that many parks in that state require you to complete a bear safety training session before they issue you a backcountry permit.

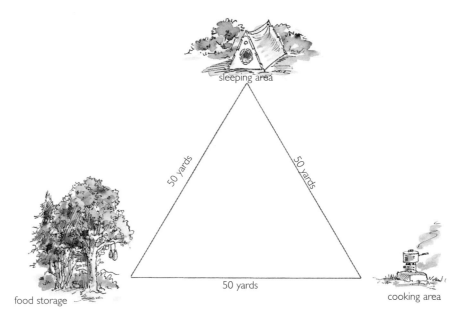

sleeping area

50 yards

50 yards

50 yards

food storage

cooking area

Form a triangle between your cooking area, sleeping area, and food storage area.

Compared to black bears, grizzlies have a characteristic hump on their shoulders and a more "dished" profile. Make noise when traveling through grizzly territory. Avoid camping along a well-traveled bear path or near a bear food source, such as a berry patch or a river with abundant salmon. If you do encounter a grizzly bear, do not act aggressively and do not turn and run. Talk to it calmly and back away. If the bear follows, stop. Most likely, if the bear charges you, it will veer off at the last moment. If you are approached, don't fight back. Instead, drop into a fetal position and play dead.

The most effective defense against either a black bear or grizzly bear attack is a pepper spray called Counter Assault. A canister costs about $42. But if you are traveling among bears, it is an excellent security blanket and may be your last line of defense. Counter Assault is sold in some outfitter and hardware stores, or you can order it from Counter Assault, PO Box 4721, Missoula, Montana, 59806, 1-800-695-3394.

To prevent an encounter with a bear, maintain a clean camp. Set up your cooking area, sleeping area, and food-storage area so these three areas form a triangle. Clean the cooking area thoroughly and store all food, garbage, and toiletries at least 50 yards from your tent (proper food storage techniques are outlined in Chapter 6). Never keep food or scented items like toothpaste in your tent. Don't burn or bury garbage: Bears will dig it up.

HUNTERS

Many areas that are open to hikers are simultaneously open to hunters. Before you plan a back-packing trip, find out if it is hunting season in the area. If so, know what is being hunted. If you are told that it is dangerous to hike in that area, heed the warning. Plan your trip elsewhere or reschedule when the hunters are gone. If the density of hunters is relatively low, you can still have a safe, rewarding trip if you follow the necessary precautions.

- Wear blaze orange. Wear hats, vests, or shirts, and strap the orange fabric on your backpack.

- Stay on the trail. If you are forced to bushwhack, talk loudly to let hunters know that you are a person.

- Be aware of what is being hunted. If you see that animal, a hunter may be near and poised to shoot. Make noise to let the hunter know you are present.

Once I was hiking through Virginia during turkey hunting season. At camp that evening I expressed my concern to another hiker about walking in such close proximity to so many hunters. His reply was terse: "If you hear a gobbler gobbling, duck!" he said. Needless to say, I was not at all comforted!

PERSONAL SAFETY

Of the many women I queried for this book, very few said they felt comfortable backpacking alone. Linda Bennett, age 34, echoed the comments of many: "I have always liked solo hiking and backpacking, but I no longer do solo trips because of two fears—an incapacitating injury in the backcountry, and the threat of attack or violence from nonhikers on the trail. If I go backpacking with a girlfriend, we are very careful to not appear 'alone' traveling to the trailhead or when hiking the trail."

Joni Clark, age 39, suggests that "adventuring, especially alone, is not fostered in women in our culture. Believing in our own capabilities, trusting our intuitions, and feeling strong and confident don't always come easy for women." The more experience you have, the more comfortable you will feel in the backcountry—alone or with a group. And as Jane Keeney, age 40, adds, "The most frightening thing in the woods is usually my imagination."

> "I stayed alone one night on the Appalachian Trail. I survived, but I usually hike with a group or someone else. I do not always hike all day with other people, but I usually camp with them."
>
> –Kathy Kelly Borowski, age 37

Attacks on female backpackers in the backcountry have occurred. But that is no reason to prevent you from enjoying the woods. Backpacking alone may be dangerous for a variety of reasons, but a solo trip can also be extremely fulfilling.

It is my philosophy that the odds of something bad happening to you are hundreds of times greater in an urban setting than they are in the wilderness. I also believe that in densely populated areas, as in many of the eastern states, trails are very accessible. Violent acts are almost always committed by nonhikers, and the dense network of roads in the East gives delinquents easy access to wilderness. I personally would think twice about traveling alone in those types of areas. But in sparsely populated areas, as in many western states, you are more likely to run into a bear than an aggressive human. I am not at all afraid of people in remote areas and have enjoyed many solo trips. If you want to hike alone but you still want the comfort of another creature, consider bringing a dog. They can be terrific companions and make you feel safer.

If you want to take your dog backpacking, there are a few things you should keep in mind. Your dog will need a doggie pack to carry his or her own food, bowls, and leash. The dog must be under strict voice control at all times, especially when there is wildlife in the area. You must understand that not everyone likes your dog as much as you do, so keep your dog from disturbing other people's camps, from stealing food, and from muddying and drinking out of the water source. Dogs are not allowed on trails in most National Parks. Check ahead of time to make sure dogs are welcome at your backpacking destination. It is also a good idea to discuss an extended trip with your veterinarian. Your dog may need special pills, including antibiotics, before embarking on a long trip.

To have the safest trip possible, give someone your itinerary listing where you plan to camp each night and when you expect to return. When you are on the trail, trust your instincts. If someone or something makes you feel uncomfortable, remove yourself from the situation. Don't tell strangers where you plan to camp. You can make polite generalizations, but don't give a stranger your travel plans. You may feel safer if you carry something to protect you. Pepper spray or mace will do the job. If you plan to carry such a defense, carry it in a holster or fanny pack and make it readily accessible in your tent. It is of no use to you if you can't get to it in seconds.

One defense I strongly urge you *not* to bring is a gun. Weapons of that magnitude have no place in a backpack.

If you travel alone, bring a plastic whistle to use if you are immobile and need help. A whistle lasts longer than your voice, and the sound carries farther. You may also want to bring a half-dozen small flares to use to signal for help if you need to be rescued. Generating smoke from a fire is another way to signal a helicopter that may be trying to locate you from above.

Another option for a safe backpacking trip is to travel in a group. Three or four women traveling together is a good-sized group. A criminal is less likely to attack a group than a single individual. And if someone gets injured, one person can stay with the victim while one or two people go for help. You can also share equipment and distribute the weight among the group to make everyone's pack a little lighter.

I have never found an activity that brings people together as well as backpacking does. Groups are good for companionship and laughs. It is comforting to share the struggle of a tough climb and the joy of a swim in a crystal lake. When you experience these things alone, it's an equally rewarding experience—but you come back feeling like you have a big secret that no one else would understand.

When traveling with others, don't let the size of the group give you a false sense of security. Be as cautious as you would if you were traveling alone. Don't let one person lead a group of blind followers; every member should be involved in making decisions. Check each other's gear, help each other across streams, and share the chores and the responsibilities of planning the route. Experience wilderness with a group and have a safe and fabulous time.

COMFORTS OF HOME

Backpacking makes you realize what makes you comfortable. It teaches you how to be resourceful to achieve the level of comfort you desire. Being comfortable is an important part of life on the trail; if you are too miserable and wet to enjoy the scenery, then it's not worth it. Most comfort comes with choosing the appropriate clothes, gear, and food for your trip. While many people get carried away with luxuries and bring too many unnecessary items, making their pack harder to carry, a few amenities that make your trip more enjoyable will be worth the weight.

REPAIR KIT

Especially on longer hikes, there is a chance that your gear may give out. The most common wounds to your equipment are tears and holes that can easily be patched with a basic repair kit. Your kit should contain the following:

- ripstop nylon tape or duct tape for patching gear or holding things together
- needle, heavy-duty thread, and a patch
- safety pins
- small pocket knife
- 50 feet of parachute cord to use not only when crossing rivers and hanging food, but also for drying clothes and as spare shoe laces

(continued on page 103)

Headlamp, candle lantern, candle, flashlight

One item that can be a necessity as well as a luxury is light. Even if you never plan on hiking or setting up camp in the dark, it happens—and it can be dangerous if you are unprepared. Your choice of light boils down to four options: a flashlight, headlamp, lantern, or candle.

Small flashlights are lightweight but difficult to hold while pitching a tent or cooking a meal. If you are backpacking with other people, someone can hold the light while the other person works. You can also hold the light in your mouth. This problem of using your hand to hold the light was solved with the headlamp. Securely mounted on your head, these lamps let you work or walk with your hands free. Both flashlights and headlamps should turn on and off by twisting the lamp, instead of flipping an actual on/off switch. Switches can turn on when jostled in your pack; then when you need your light, the batteries are dead. Depending on how often you plan on using your light, you may want to carry spare batteries.

Lanterns and candles are good for diffused light once you're settled in camp. Small candle lanterns or oil lanterns can easily light up a tent or shelter. Putting a metallic wind screen behind a small candle generates enough light to read, write, or play games. Never leave a flame unattended, and never use candles inside your flammable tent. On any surface, use a candle that is short and fat and set it in a holder. An empty sardine or tuna can works well.

Items that I never leave behind are a camera, paper, and pencil. I take pictures often and try to write a journal entry each night to fully document my trip. My photo albums and journals are my most valued possessions. They remind me of exciting times and delightful moments that would otherwise escape my memory.

If you have a nice camera, keep it in a water resistant, well-padded case. If you are concerned about damaging expensive camera equipment, carry a disposable camera in a Ziploc bag instead. It will be extremely light and will take surprisingly great pictures, and you don't have to worry about damaging it.

A small notebook in a plastic bag makes a fine journal. Your journal might be a technical document—how many miles you traveled, where you camped, the temperature, your pace, etc. Or it might contain descriptive passages about what you've seen, how you felt, and whatever else nature inspires you to write. I can't stress enough how much fun it is to reread journals and relive trips. Once writing becomes a habit, it is easy to do. On longer trips, I carry extra paper, a few envelopes, and stamps for writing letters.

When you're traveling with a group, a game or deck of cards can provide good entertainment. A miniature deck of cards weighs very little. I find that on group trips I play card games quite often. Travel guides and books that help you identify wildflowers or birds can also be fun to bring. If you are with a few people, you can each carry a different book and someone can carry binoculars. Some people like to carry binoculars at all times to scope out the trail. I have never had any need for binoculars: Mine only get used on day hikes or when I'm birding.

There are a number of less essential items you might consider bringing. Some people like to carry a paperback book or a Walkman. Others feel something like a radio detracts from the wilderness experience.

The final items that should find their way into your pack are a little money and identification, such as a driver's license. If you finish your trip in a town, you can run into a store and get that cold drink you've been dreaming about for days. Finally, you may want to carry a watch, which can help you determine your pace, figure out how much daylight you have left, and keep track of what time you need to get to town to catch a bus or go to the post office. Most of the time when hiking I'd rather not know what time it is. I usually keep my watch hidden in my pack.

REPAIR KIT

(continued from page 102)

Most holes and tears in your clothing and equipment can be temporarily patched with ripstop tape or duct tape. On longer trips, sewing a patch over a tear is a more permanent solution. Patches for most gear—such as tents, sleeping bags, and backpacks—should be made of a durable, ripstop, water-repellent material. Use safety pins as a quick fix for broken straps or torn clothing that you'd rather sew when you get home. Parachute cord also has a number of uses; it makes a quick repair for broken shoe laces. Cut the cord to the appropriate length, and then burn the cut ends with a lighter or match to glue the ends so they won't unravel.

HYGIENE

Personal maintenance kit

Just how *do* you do those things like bathing and grooming in the woods? People who have never backpacked before always express interest in the hows and wheres of these procedures. Hygiene is a topic that deserves careful consideration. Keep the contents of your personal maintenance kit in a Ziploc freezer bag. Keep the number of items to a minimum. Things to include are:

- toothbrush
- toothpaste, tiny tube
- comb
- biodegradable soap (but see note, below)
- pack towel
- sunscreen
- lip balm with sun protection
- tampons, pads, or any other device to catch menstrual flow
- moist wipes
- extra Ziploc bags and cloth bag
- toilet paper (partial roll)

A toothbrush is necessary; the handle is optional. Save weight by carrying only the amount of toothpaste you need. Buy the tiny sample tubes or bring a partially used tube.

A tiny comb is lighter than a brush—and when you think about it, it's not really necessary to do much with your hair. I like to run a comb through my hair on long trips to keep from getting dreadlocks and to look somewhat presentable when hitching into town. I wear my hair in a pony tail or in braids most of the time, or I hide it under a baseball cap or a bandanna.

When it comes right down to it, soap is not necessary. It pollutes the environment; even biodegradable soaps cannot biodegrade in water. If you insist on using soap, do not bring the bar of soap that's in your shower. You can use the same biodegradable soap you use for your dishes. Most of these soaps are multipurpose, appropriate for dishes, your body, brushing teeth, and washing hair. I have used the soap for all these purposes. Brushing your teeth with it is not an enjoyable experience—the taste is horrendous, so I stick with regular toothpaste. It is my feeling that you should use the biodegradable soap for dishes and never do more than rinse your body with

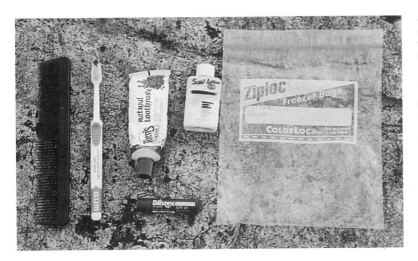

Contents of a personal mainte-nance kit. I like to keep tampons, pads, toilet paper, wipes, and extra bags separate from the other toiletries.

water on the trail. Save the soapy shower until you get back home. And there is no reason to wash your hair on the trail. It's extremely difficult when you can't dunk your soapy head in a stream (remember, never put any soap in or near the water).

The list includes a towel—and I don't mean your big bath towel. Some people like to bring a flannel pack towel, which has an area of about a square foot. The material should be readily absorbent and quick drying. You can wring most of the water out of a pack towel and then attach it to your pack to dry. Since most backpacking clothes are water resistant and are designed not to retain water, it is nice to have one item that does absorb water. A bandanna makes a good towel, as does a cotton T-shirt.

Sunscreen and lip balm are essential on nearly all excursions. Use a high SPF lotion and apply it often, especially to delicate exposed areas like your nose, ears, neck, and shoulders.

Bathing and brushing

On a scorcher, there is nothing more refreshing than jumping into a cool lake. As a backpacker you have earned the right to such luxuries! You should, however, wipe off bug repellent and sunscreen before you intoxicate the swimmers and skidders whose home you are bathing in. Fill a bottle, bag, or pot with water; walk away from the water source, and rinse off. Scatter the dirty water at least 200 feet from the source.

If the stream or lake water is too cold, you can take a warm shower if the sun is out and if you have a water bag. Fill your bag and let it soak up the sun on a dark surface for an hour or two. Hang the bag from a tree, open the spout, and take a quick, warm shower. You can also carry pots of water away from the water source, add a little soap if you must, and

A water bag can serve as a shower.

wash off. Dispose of soapy water at least 200 feet from the water source and make sure not to dump it into a drainage ditch or an obvious runoff path. If you don't dispose of your waste water correctly, the next rain will wash your soap into the stream or lake.

I have never actually taken a full-fledged shower in the wilderness. I've found that once you get past a certain level of dirtiness, you don't mind anymore. It is not essential that you bathe on the trail; however, you should wash your hands and face every day. When you do, use treated water. If water is limited, bring a couple antiseptic towelettes to wipe your hands, especially after going to the bathroom. Remember, the nasty little parasite *Giardia* is spread through fecal-oral contamination.

When you brush your teeth, use only treated water and spit well away from the water source and your camping area. The fact that bears are attracted to the scent of toothpaste should be extra incentive to brush your teeth far from camp.

If after a few days your socks and underwear become crusty and you refuse to put them near your body, you may have to give them a thorough rinsing. If you decide to wash socks, underwear, or anything that has sunscreen or bug repellent on it, knead the clothes in a pot or in a plastic bag. Retrieve water from the source for washing and rinsing and dispose of dirty water 200 feet from the source. If your shirts and pants are just dirty from dust and sweat, you can rinse them out in a fast flowing stream. Avoid using soap, and avoid using areas like small alpine lakes or shallow, clear streams for washing. These areas may be too fragile to handle much human disturbance.

SANITATION

Number one

Deciding where to relieve yourself requires a little foresight. If you only need to pee, make sure you are 150 feet from a trail, water source, or from a slope or drainage that feeds into a water source. At camp, walk at least 150 feet from your sleeping and cooking areas. Urine is virtually sterile, but it's nice not to have the stench of urine wafting by as you're cooking dinner or trying to get to sleep.

Peeing in the woods is a skill you want to master. There are a couple ways to do it. I prefer the basic squat—unclasp your hip belt, drop your pants, spread your legs, and squat down. To minimize the splatter on your boots, put your feet on rocks or logs, which will elevate them, and pee in the gap between. I found that peeing with your pack on is easy if you have thigh muscles strong enough to support the weight. Toward the end of the day when your legs are getting tired, you may not have the energy to hold a squat position for very long. The solution: Stand in front of a tree and, as you lower yourself down, hold onto the trunk for support. Lean back and take the weight off your legs.

This discussion of peeing with your pack on may sound silly. But when you are sweaty and the air is cold, the last thing you want to do is remove your backpack. When you remount the pack, the sweat on your pack and your back will have begun to freeze, and you will have to press an icy pack against your damp skin. This is no fun.

Some women have mastered the skill of peeing while standing upright. This saves the strain on your thighs, but it takes some practice to not dampen anything except the ground. It is a bit of a procedure to slide your shorts down with your pack on. Baggy shorts may be the answer.

Number two

More planning is required when you have to do more than pee. It's important that you follow these procedures for proper waste disposal to prevent our waters from becoming contaminated, to ensure that people and animals don't encounter your waste, and to speed the rate at which fecal matter decomposes.

Your poop site should be 200 feet from a water source—again, in a place that will not drain into water during the next storm. There are two ways to do it, depending on where you are. If you are traveling in a remote area where there are few, if any, signs of other people, you should poop on a rock. Then with a stick, smear the poop on the rock in a thin layer. The sun will dry it out and it will flake off and decompose much faster than if you bury it. The smear works extremely well in dry climates.

If you are in a heavily used area, it may not be appropriate for everyone to smear all the rocks in sight. In this case, you should bury the poop. Use either the heel of your boot or a plastic or metal trowel and dig a hole about six inches deep. Poop in the hole, then take a stick and mix up the poop with the surrounding soil so bacteria that decompose fecal matter can get straight to work. Fill in the hole and scatter leaves or rocks on top to disguise it.

If you are traveling in snowy conditions, you must carry a few extra Ziploc bags and pack out your poop. Otherwise the ground will be covered with fecal matter in the spring, and the piles of poop will have a better chance of being carried to a water source with the melting snow.

Toilet paper is another matter. Too often, I've seen toilet areas at popular campsites littered with toilet paper that has escaped from hikers' shallow holes. Never bury toilet paper; it must be packed out. Carry a Ziploc bag for this purpose. It used to be acceptable to burn toilet paper, but the high incidence of fire in the last decade has made people wary of this method. If you have a controlled campfire, though, and if your companions don't object, you can burn your used paper there. Keep in mind that packing it out is the preferred and most environmentally sound method.

When you get home, dispose of your used toilet paper in the toilet. Contaminated paper cannot end up in a landfill; it must go through your waste water treatment plant or septic system. The bag can be washed and reused on your next trip. Of course, you can avoid this entire ordeal by using natural toilet paper. Leaves, sticks, and snow work well. Be aware of where you squat—you don't want to end up in a patch of poison ivy or stinging nettle. Know the poisonous plants in the area you're traveling.

• •

"**I** was hesitant about going to the bathroom outdoors and also the possibility of having my period while backpacking. This is something you overcome the more you do it. It isn't a drawback if you are prepared and have a separate trash bag for used sanitary products. If you have an opaque cloth bag inside a plastic bag, you know just where to put used products and you don't have to look at them because they're in a cloth bag."

—Helen Gentile, age 37

• •

Number three

When I go backpacking I always carry a few tampons, even if I don't expect to get my period. When you are days from the nearest drug store, it is better to play it safe. I learned the hard way.

When you are menstruating while on the trail, carry an extra bag to store used tampons, pads, and their wrappers. To avoid attracting animals at camp, hang or store used tampons and pads as you would store food and other toiletries (proper storage is discussed in Chapter 6). Never bury these items; they pollute the environment and invite animals to dig them up. Also, don't dispose of them in backcountry outhouses. They do not aid in the natural decomposition process, and they have to be removed by hand when the outhouse is cleaned. Volunteers usually clean outhouses. It's not a fun job to begin with, so don't make it any more difficult for people who volunteer their weekends maintaining trails and facilities.

To feel a little cleaner, I like to carry premoistened cloths like baby wipes or antiseptic towelettes instead of toilet paper. Of course, these must be packed out as well. One Colorado woman, age 39, suggests a creative technique for dealing with your period.

"I use my diaphragm to 'catch' menstrual flow. The blood is non-polluting when poured into the soil and when washing up in a stream. It's so much easier than messing with used tampons or pads."

Menstrual cups, diaphragms, sponges, and any other devices that catch menstrual flow may work well for you. It is really a matter of personal preference and what method you feel most comfortable with.

Instead of thinking of your period as a curse, think of it as a blessing in disguise. It is a symbol of your ability to give life, a sacred ability unique to women. It is something to cherish and endure—even in the woods.

Chapter 8

WHERE TO GO BACKPACKING

When you think about going backpacking, do you picture yourself climbing steep mountains or strolling through meadows? Sleeping beneath a thick canopy of trees or under the stars? Making coffee on a chilly morning or swigging down a quart of water as the sun scorches the desert sands?

Every backpacker has a favorite scenario for adventure and exploration. But there are unlimited places to backpack, so how can you narrow the options and choose just one place?

Select a backpacking destination by considering your goals, the length of time you have, the difficulty and length of the trail, and the type of environment you prefer to be in.

"**M**y favorite trips are annual week-long treks we take into the high Sierra Nevada range where we meet few other people. The remoteness and beauty and pride of achievement all make me so happy and privileged to be there, to be human."

—Liz Miller, age 45

FAVORITE DESTINATIONS
• • • • • • • • • • • • • • • • • • •

My favorite backpacking destination is anywhere that I can
climb above treeline and see
wide open spaces. The mountains hold something magical
for me. When my face hits
mountain air, I am instantly
energized. There is no place
I am happier.

Your favorite backpacking
memory may turn out to be a
solo trip along a coast, a trek
with your girlfriends through
the hills of the Southeast,
or a romantic getaway to the
canyonlands of Utah. Or your
favorite destination might
change every year. It might
be across the country or just
beyond your doorstep. That is
the magic of backpacking: The
weather conditions, your state
of mind, and your companions
change with every trip, providing you with unique adventures
every time you set out. You
can find the extraordinary and
stunning in unfamiliar places
or in places you might have
visited a hundred times.

PLANNING YOUR TRIP

When I plan a backpacking trip, I pick the general location first.
This may be as big a place as Glacier National Park in Montana or
a small area like the trails near my house. I determine how much
time I have to backpack. Then I get my hands on a map.

When I planned a trip to Glacier, I called the park headquarters and left a message requesting backcountry information
and trail maps. I received all the information a couple weeks later.
I found a trail that I could comfortably hike in three days, called a
friend who had spent a considerable amount of time in the park,
and had her verify that my choice was a good route for three days
of travel in July.

Some parks such as Glacier National Park and Shenendoah
National Park in Virginia require that you register for a backcountry permit and provide them with your itinerary. (You should probably leave an itinerary even if they don't require it.) Reservations
for campsites or shelters often get filled early in the season, so it is
a good idea to contact the park for information about permits and
reservations as soon as you decide to plan a trip.

Public lands are excellent places to go backpacking, and information about trails that run through parks is easy to obtain. Call the
park or send a postcard to request general park information and
maps that show hiking trails. If you want to explore national forests,
wilderness areas, or Bureau of Land Manage-ment (BLM) areas,
contact the U.S.D.A. Forest Service (see the Resource Directory,
page 137, for addresses), or the chamber of commerce in a town near
those areas. You should be able to obtain a pamphlet on local trails
or recommendations on maps and trail guides.

Hardware and sporting goods stores usually sell topographic
maps (maps that show the contours of the land) and maps of trails
in the vicinity. Another option is to talk to employees at local outdoor outfitting stores. They should be familiar with the area, be
able to give you advice about certain hikes, recommend a trip to
suit your ability and the length of time you have, inform you about
present trail conditions, give you directions to trail heads, and offer other tips about backpacking.
An excellent book that can help you decide where to go is *The Essential Guide to Hiking in the
U.S.: All Major Trails and Hiking Areas Including National and State Parks, Forests and Preserves* by
Charles Cook (see the Resource Directory).

Plan where you will camp each night and calculate the number of miles you'll have to hike each day. I generally like to take it easy the first day to give myself a chance to get acclimated to backpacking. I like to hike around eight miles the first day, although the mileage you travel ultimately depends on the terrain and how fit you are. Your pack is heaviest when you begin a trip, so plan to cover fewer miles until you eat one to two days' worth of food.

Once you've studied the map and you have chosen a prospective route, talk to someone who has hiked that route or spent time in the general area. This can be a friend, a person at the local outfitting store, or a ranger. If you are traveling to a park, definitely talk to a ranger about your trip. He or she will be happy to give you the information that the maps don't contain, including if your chosen route is an appropriate length for the time you've allotted. Park employees can also fill you in on the current weather and trail conditions, recommend certain campsites, suggest a place to park your car, and let you know about any precautions to take or special gear to bring. They'll be aware of local floods, forest fires, or snow conditions that affect the trail.

On my Appalachian Trail through-hike, I was advised to stay at my camp for a day while firefighters subdued a fire on the Virginia–West Virginia border, just a mile north of my camp. Two months later, I met rangers in Maine who were stationed at a river crossing. It happened to be the wettest summer in Maine since the turn of the century, and the rivers were wild and frothy and streaked with dangerously swift currents. Since there are no bridges on the Appalachian Trail in Maine (all bridges that were built were subsequently washed away in spring floods), rangers directed me to a network of logging roads so I could bypass the treacherous ford.

If you had been planning a trip through those areas and had contacted the Forest Service, you would have been forewarned about the forest fire and the floods before you began your trip. Knowing these things ahead of time can ensure that your hike is a safe one and save you the agony of rerouting your trip.

In addition to the previously mentioned public lands, there are eight National Scenic Trails and a handful of other long-distance trails. The more popular ones include: the Appalachian Trail from Georgia to Maine; the Long Trail from Vermont to Canada; the Colorado Trail; the John Muir Trail in California; and the Pacific Crest Trail from Mexico to Canada (for more on long-distance trails, see Chapter 11).

Most people who hike these trails do not attempt to hike the entire trail; they are great for weekend trips and short expeditions. Most people live closer to a long-distance trail than they think. For example, three-fourths of the population of the United States lives within a day's drive of the Appalachian Trail! Find the section of trail closest to you and head out for a few days. You may find it addicting and soon find yourself planning to hike the entire trail. I have seen it happen before!

FOREST, DESERT, AND ALPINE ENVIRONMENTS

If you are still not sure where you want to backpack, consider three major environments: forest, desert, and alpine (loosely defined as above the treeline). The time of year you hike will often

Shade and water are the most important considerations on a desert backpack. (Photo by Cliff Leight)

determine what environment you need to prepare for. For example, if you backpack in a forest environment in the winter, you may use alpine and winter camping equipment and techniques. If you backpack in a desert environment in the summer, you will need to be more concerned about shade and water than if you hiked the same area in the winter.

Most people, especially beginners, backpack in what I consider a forest or mountain environment. The information in this book pertains mostly to this type of backpacking. However, you should be aware of the other types of backpacking. If you plan a trip through a desert region or through a mountainous region above treeline, you'll need to be familiar with some additional facets of backpacking.

Desert backpacking

The desert backpacking experience is unique and rewarding. If you haven't spent much time in a desert, you will be amazed by the unusual wildlife and exotic plants that are found in these arid environments. Weather is predictable and usually hot, which means you won't have to carry as much weight as you would in a colder, wetter climate.

The two most important considerations of desert traveling are water and shade. You may need to carry more water in the desert than you would in a forest. Call the Forest Service or Park Service to get information about the abundance and quality of water holes. Shade may also be difficult to find. Sunscreen and appropriate clothing are critical elements of desert traveling. Wear thin, light-colored, long-sleeve shirts, sunglasses with ultraviolet (UV) protection, and a light sun hat. Some outfitting stores sell UV shirts that block the sun's harmful rays. If you do not wear a UV shirt, wear sunscreen under your garments, as the sun's rays can penetrate other types of clothing.

You can cut weight by carrying light clothes and a light tent. To avoid bugs, many backpackers prefer to carry a lightweight tent instead of sleeping under the stars. A well-ventilated tent or a mesh tent is ideal. Before you begin a hike in the desert, it is important to be able to recognize the symptoms of heat exhaustion and know how to treat it. Scorpions and snakes pose an additional threat to the desert backpacker. But you can take simple precautions, such as shaking out your clothes and boots every morning, to avoid coming in contact with these critters (see Chapter 7 for more on backpacking safety). If you want to learn more about desert backpacking, read *Desert Hiking* by Dave Ganci (see the Resource Directory, page 137).

Alpine backpacking and winter camping

Alpine backpacking and winter camping are at the opposite end of the spectrum from desert trekking. Instead of worrying about how to stay cool, you need to figure out how to stay warm. Weather is often unpredictable in alpine environments. Storm clouds can very quickly ambush a clear, sunny day. When hiking in these areas, be prepared for strong sun, high winds, rain, sleet, hail, and snow. Because of these varied conditions, your pack may weigh a little more than you'd like. But in an alpine environment, it is better to be prepared for anything.

If you are hiking in snow, waterproof boots will make your trip more comfortable and more safe. You will also want to invest in a pair of gaiters. Gaiters will help keep snow and rocks out of your boots (see page 53 for more on gaiters).

Wear many layers of warm clothes under a waterproof outer layer. The most effective layering system includes a silk or synthetic layer, a lightweight fleece, and a heavy fleece or wool sweater. (For a further discussion of layering, see page 50.) Gloves and a hat are a must. It is critical that you keep a set of clothes, especially socks, dry at all times—even if it means changing into cold, damp clothes in the morning. If you don't have dry clothes to change into at night, you may risk suffering from hypothermia or frostbite. I recommend carrying everything in waterproof stuff sacks or Ziploc bags.

I began my Appalachian Trail hike in February and encountered more than my fair share of snow. There were many mornings when a passerby could have heard me shrieking as I slipped my damp, icy "day shirt" over my head. I usually warmed up in about 5 to 10 minutes. But at the end of each day I changed into my dry "night shirt"—and I reconfirmed that a warm, dry shirt was well worth the morning's shrieks!

You also need to carry a four-season tent, which is specifically designed to keep you warm and maintain its structure in inclement weather. The temperature rating and the filling of your sleeping bag warrant careful consideration (for more on sleeping bags, see page 47). The temperature rating of your sleeping bag should match the lowest temperature you expect to encounter. A zero-degree sleeping bag should suffice for the majority of alpine excursions. For extra warmth and dryness, a vapor barrier liner can be fitted into your bag. Such a liner can add as much as 20 degrees to the temperature rating of your sleeping bag. You also want to make sure you have ample room in the bottom of your bag to store a water jug, a camera,

Taking backpacking to the extreme—alpine or mountaineering excursions pose new challenges. (Photo by Cliff Leight)

• •

"I read a book about how to build a snow cave, and I bought a shovel the next week. The author said that in twenty years he'd never slept cold in a snow cave—that was encouraging. My first snow cave was no work of art—it was a little lopsided and I messed up the entrance, but there was something so wonderful about sleeping inside the snow. It was so quiet and dark. I thought, This is really something. This is what experiencing nature is all about."

—Laurie Ehlers, age 29

• •

your boots, and anything else that you'd like to prevent from freezing during the night.

Because your body will burn more calories as it tries to keep warm on an alpine adventure, you need to bring more food. You may also want to carry extra fuel so you can cook more hot meals. When you are caught in cold rain or snow, there are few things that you will want more than a hot meal. A hot cup of tea or soup is often the best way to fight a chill.

If all this talk of being cold and wet sounds like a dreadful experience, think again. If you are prepared, you will reap the rewards of winter camping. The solitude and peace of winter are unmatched in any other season. Hikers often crowd popular trails in the warmer months. But in the winter, you may have the trail to yourself. You also don't have to worry about bugs and bears—a major bonus. Your water will stay cold while you walk. And if the ground is covered in snow, you have a water source at your feet. Instead of searching out a river or spring, just melt the snow with your stove. Bring the water to a boil to purify it. (Water treatment techniques are discussed in detail in Chapter 6, pages 80–83.)

If you hike in winter conditions, it is important to learn about avalanche safety. You should learn how to dig a snow pit to test the stability of the snow, how to build snow caves to sleep in, and how to dig fire pits for cooking. You may want to know how to use snowshoes, crampons, and an ice ax and learn how to read a map and compass.

As you become a more experienced backpacker, you may want to investigate techniques for backpacking under these more advanced conditions. Some great books on alpine backpacking and winter camping are listed in the "Go farther" section of the Resource Directory, page 137.

Chapter 9

🚶 LOVING THE LAND: LOW-IMPACT BACKPACKING

Nothing is more inspiring and more sacred than the natural world—and nothing is in as much danger of being destroyed. Backpackers typically have an inherent interest in preserving the earth. But even if people have good intentions, they may not realize the impact of their actions on the environment.

Low-impact backpacking includes a set of techniques that help minimize signs of your visits to natural places. The first step in practicing low-impact techniques is to become aware of the consequences of everything you do. That means considering the consequences of how you walk to a water source, where you pitch your tent, how you dispose of waste, how you clean yourself, and how you act around animals. Once you become aware of your actions, you can modify them so you impose as little strain as possible on the environment. As backpackers, we need to make every effort to leave the water, land, plants, and animals as we found them if we want the areas we travel to remain unspoiled and open.

The National Outdoor Leadership School (NOLS) has led a strong campaign to educate campers and hikers on low-impact techniques. For information about their Leave No Trace program, or for information on treading lightly in desert and alpine environments, contact NOLS. For contact information see the Resource Directory, page 137; check out the books under "Go lightly," page 139, as well.

MINIMUM-IMPACT GUIDELINES

- Stay on designated trails.
- Do not cut switchbacks.
- Choose an established, legal campsite that is 200 feet from trails and water.
- Do not build structures or dig trenches.
- Wash dishes, clothes, and your body 200 feet from water.
- Deposit human waste in holes that are 4 to 8 inches deep and at least 200 feet from water.
- Pack out toilet paper.
- Leave plants, feathers, rocks, etc., as you found them.
- Control pets at all times.
- Pack out all trash and left-over food.

Delicate environments like the area around this high-elevation pond are in danger of being destroyed by campers who don't practice minimum-impact techniques.

DELICATE ECOSYSTEMS

A major concern to environmentalists is the issue of human impact on delicate ecosystems. Sensitive environments such as high alpine tundras and ponds, steep canyons, and remote wetlands support threatened and endangered plants and animals. Because of the beauty and isolation of these places, they may also be attractive to backpackers. The result is that people flock to these ecosystems and—although they mean well—end up loving the land to death.

Land managers and private organizations have realized that this scenario is becoming a reality in many delicate places. Colorado's Fourteeners—54 peaks that rise above 14,000 feet—are a good example. It has become increasingly popular to attempt to climb all the Fourteeners. As a result, these fragile alpine environments—many of which contain rare plants—are being trampled on and destroyed. Managers have started to create trails up once trail-less peaks and mark areas that are more sensitive to disturbance.

A similar scenario has been played out on Mt. Everest, the highest mountain in the world. During the past decade, the mountain has seen a dramatic increase in the number of people who attempt to ascend it. During their efforts to reach the 29,028-foot summit, climbers are often faced with life-threatening conditions. During these times, proper disposal of trash, excrement, and dead bodies is generally ignored. Thousands of pounds of trash have been left up on the mountain, especially at Base Camp. Realizing the threat to this ecosystem, the Nepalese government has instituted higher fees in an attempt to limit the number of visitors. (One climber can pay $65,000 or more for a permit to ascend higher than Base Camp.) And starting in 1996, expeditions were required to haul out a certain amount of trash or their $4,000 deposit would be withheld. The trash on the mountain is diminishing. But sadly, the number of visitors has not declined, and Mt. Everest has become a challenge only for people who can shell out big bucks.

Because of the devastating impact of too many people in fragile ecosystems, such areas may be restricted and higher fees may be charged to gain access. Many of our national parks already limit the number of backcountry permits they issue, and fees to enter parks are rising. To prevent being shut out from wilderness areas or having our wallets drained, as backpackers we have the responsibility to show land managers that we can use these delicate areas without destroying them. If we recognize fragile places and practice minimum-impact techniques, we will be able to enjoy these special places for generations to come.

One person or group can make a difference. If you pass your knowledge on to others and encourage them to do the same, information on minimum-impact techniques will spread quickly. If you see someone washing soapy dishes in a mountain stream, let her know she is polluting the water and show her the proper technique (outlined on pages 86–87). Nearly all the backpackers I've met genuinely want to protect the environment, and they welcome advice that will help them tread more lightly.

Delicate ecosystems are often fragile because of severe climatic conditions. They may be situated on an exposed, windy ridge or at a high elevation, or they might be fed by a small amount of water. Small alpine ponds or streams may not recover from the soap residue or bug repellent that people might put in them. These ecosystems cannot recover from disturbances as easily as hardier environments such as low-elevation forests or large, muddy rivers. Treat these delicate places with care.

> It does take some guts to go up to someone and tell them they're hurting the environment. But they usually appreciate it; they usually just didn't know it was wrong.

When you are walking through a fragile environment, stay on the trails so you don't trample rare species and the fragile land that surrounds water. When possible, step on rocks or snow instead of on soil or water. Don't wash your hands in the water if you have sunscreen or repellent on them. Never wash clothes or cookware in such water sources, and relieve yourself at least 200 feet from the source. And don't remove or relocate anything (plants, animals, rocks, etc.) from its present location.

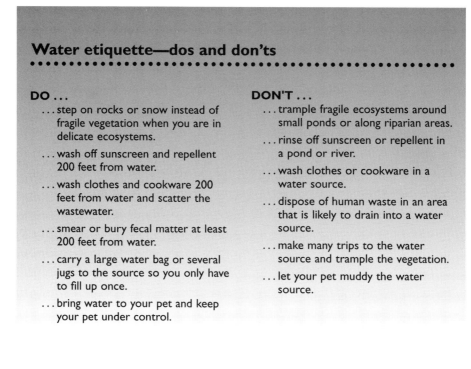

Water etiquette—dos and don'ts

DO ...

...step on rocks or snow instead of fragile vegetation when you are in delicate ecosystems.

...wash off sunscreen and repellent 200 feet from water.

...wash clothes and cookware 200 feet from water and scatter the wastewater.

...smear or bury fecal matter at least 200 feet from water.

...carry a large water bag or several jugs to the source so you only have to fill up once.

...bring water to your pet and keep your pet under control.

DON'T ...

...trample fragile ecosystems around small ponds or along riparian areas.

...rinse off sunscreen or repellent in a pond or river.

...wash clothes or cookware in a water source.

...dispose of human waste in an area that is likely to drain into a water source.

...make many trips to the water source and trample the vegetation.

...let your pet muddy the water source.

WATER

You don't have to be an environmental activist to know that the world has problems with water. Examples of water degradation are all around us: the water wars in the West; the suffering economies of New England fishing villages from the overharvesting of ocean fish; the catastrophic oil spills near Kuwait and Alaska; the way we dam and dredge and destroy rivers, lakes, wetlands, and oceans. You could say that humans have polluted the pond they drink from.

Let's not do the same on a small scale. When you go backpacking, you may travel to a remote area that has escaped the type of pollution that has contaminated other water sources. Enjoy and cherish these places and work to keep them pristine—or at least no more polluted than they already are.

Waste

Proper waste disposal methods are discussed in detail in Chapter 7 (pages 106–107). The important thing to remember is that you want human waste to deteriorate as quickly as possible and without the possibility of it being carried to water. Smear or bury fecal matter at least 200 feet from water. Look for a place that will not drain into water if it rains.

Cleaning

Guidelines for cleaning yourself and your clothes are in Chapter 7 (pages 104–106) and techniques for washing dishes are discussed in Chapter 6 (pages 86–87). Again, the most important

● ●

"**N**othing is more gross than walking into someone's poop or seeing toilet paper flapping in the breeze. Be conscious of your actions. Take a little time to dispose of waste properly. Better yet, pack it out!"

—Mandy Williams, age 34

● ●

thing to consider is how to keep your wastewater away from the water source. Scatter wastewater from washing clothes, washing yourself, cleaning pots, and brushing your teeth at least 200 feet from the source. Under no circumstance should soap (even biodegradable soap) enter a water source.

When you collect water at camp to use for cleaning, cooking, and drinking, bring a water bag or many water bottles so you don't have to make several trips. If there is a designated path to the source, follow it. If not, take a route to the water that your fellow campers haven't taken. The land adjacent to a stream or surrounding a lake is called a *riparian zone*. Riparian zones are critical to the health of the stream and the wildlife in the area. But they are often fragile and can't withstand a few good tramplings. Vegetation has a better chance of recovering from one pair of boots than from ten.

LAND

Fire

Until people began to understand the devastating impact campfires can have on the environment, it was as natural to build a fire as it was to pitch a tent. We now realize how quickly a campfire can become a full-fledged, raging monster. Recently there have been many forest fires that

The **riparian zone** appears as a corridor of thick vegetation beside the river.

have burned out of control and threatened natural habitats and urban developments. Campfires also strip the land of dead wood that provides habitats for insects and small mammals. And forests rely on dead wood to naturally decay and improve the quality of the soil. Cutting down branches or trees for a fire is an obvious no-no—just as building fires next to boulders is. These techniques leave long-lasting scars on trees and soot scars on rocks.

Another reason for snuffing out campfires is that when people see a fire ring, they tend to view it as a go-ahead to dump their trash. We then end up with fire pits filled with plastic and foil that either won't burn or is polluting. For these reasons, campfires are prohibited in many fragile, dry, or heavily used areas. Before you begin your trip, inquire at a ranger station or with local officials about current fire regulations. You should never rely on a fire as your sole method for cooking since you can't always count on conditions to be adequate for a safe fire. Carry a camp stove.

Sitting around a campfire can add ambiance to any night in the wild, and it's difficult to stomp out a backcountry tradition as popular as building a campfire. There are times and techniques for building a safe campfire with minimum impact to the environment. Here are some guidelines:

1. Inquire with rangers or local officials about backcountry conditions (moisture and wind) and fire regulations.

2. Choose an area that has had minimal use. Never build a fire in a place that has been stripped of wood.

3. Use a pre-existing fire ring or fire pit. If there is more than one ring in the area, use one and dismantle the others by scattering the rocks and ashes. As a last resort, create your own fire pit by digging a shallow hole in rocky or sandy soil in an area that is void of plants and shrubs. If you use rocks, put them back where you found them once the fire is out.

4. Make sure there are no overhanging branches above the fire.

5. Use dead wood that is on the ground (never from a tree) and pieces that are no more than two inches thick. Keep your fire small and burn the wood to ash. Axes and saws should not be used: They leave scars on trees and branches.

6. Monitor the fire: Never leave it unattended.

7. Douse the fire with water until there are no hot spots. Wait at least a half-hour before you leave to ensure the fire is completely out and the ashes are cooling.

8. If you are using an established fire ring, make sure you have burned the wood to ash and the ashes are cool and soaked with water. Don't cover the fire with dirt, because the pit will fill quickly and be useless to other campers. If you are in a lightly used area, dismantle the ring, return the rocks to their original locations, and scatter the cold ashes.

Stay on the trail

There are a few low-impact guidelines to follow as you're walking.

If there is a defined path, stay on it. Trails are scars on the land, but they are there to keep

Switchbacks make it easier to climb mountains and prevent the trail from eroding.

the impact of thousands of boots to a minimum. Switchbacks, where a trail traverses back and forth, are designed to prevent the trail from eroding. If a trail went straight up a mountain, water would collect on the trail, form a little stream, and in a short time erode a trench. In Great Smoky Mountains National Park, millions of hikers' steps have eroded trails into trenches that are four feet deep. These trails generally run in a straight line and create channels in which water flows like a stream. These trails will eventually be rerouted, but they serve as an excellent example of the eroding abilities of hikers and water. Don't degrade properly designed trails into flooded channels. Don't cut the switchbacks. Stay on the trail.

After a rainstorm, parts of the trail may be flooded or muddy. Don't walk around the muddy spots. You will widen the trail by doing so. If you walk through the mud, your boots will dry soon enough. But if you walk around it, the trampled vegetation on the side of the trail may never recover.

There are two times when it is okay to leave the trail: breaks and cross-country trips. When you stop for a break, choose a durable sight like a rock slab or a spread of pine needles hidden from the trail. There is nothing more aggravating than a group of hikers who sprawl out in the middle of the trail to have a snack.

If you decide to go on a cross-country trip, where you won't be following a trail, travel with no more than four to six people. If there are more than two of you, don't walk single file. Instead, spread out to lessen the impact on the vegetation and to avoid creating a trail. Don't mark your route with string or sticks or piles of rocks. You should not leave any trace of your travels.

Pack out trash

It is the cardinal rule of backpacking to leave no trace of your travels. One of the most obvious ways to do this is to pack out every item you pack in. In addition to trash like food wrappers and Band-Aids, remember to pack out toilet paper, tampons, pads, cigarette butts, matches, and literally every piece of lint, thread, and paper you bring with you. As you plan your food for a trip, eliminate as much packaging as you can; don't take food that will leave you with bulky or heavy containers after the food has been consumed. Carry an extra bag to use exclusively for trash. I always carry the trash bag in an outside pocket on my backpack to keep it away from food and clothes. If you see trash left behind by inconsiderate hikers, do your Good Samaritan deed of the day and pack it out as well.

At camp

When you stake your claim for the night, remember that you should leave no trace of your presence when you pack up in the morning. Choose a spot that is at least 200 feet from water. Pitch the tent on a durable spot, such as a clearing of dirt, pine needles, or sturdy grasses. It's okay to move sharp rocks and sticks from your tent site, but don't clear a spot for your tent by cutting branches or shrubs or matting down wildflowers. Don't cut boughs to make a soft bed, dig a moat around the tent, or build rock walls to shield the wind. The same goes when you choose cooking and washing areas. Set your stove on dirt or on a rock and put a foil shield under the stove to prevent the fire from scarring the rock. Leave the spot exactly as you found it.

Remember that noise and bright colors are forms of pollution, too. If you are sharing a campsite with others, remain quiet. Never play music or engage in games that may vocally get out of control. If you have a bright-colored tent, conceal it behind a large tree or bush. If you bring a pet, make sure it is under control at all times.

"**W**hen everyone in my group is packed up and ready to go, we do a 'last look' to search for any sign that we spent the night. We look for anything: scraps of food, candy wrappers, trampled vegetation, rocks from a fire pit, etc. If there is no sign of our stay, we know we did it right."

—Nancy Hillerman, age 42

PLANTS AND ANIMALS

"Take only pictures and leave only footprints." This popular saying includes words to live by in the backcountry. It is illegal to remove anything from a national park without a special permit. That means it is illegal to pick flowers, collect feathers, or take rocks. If all visitors picked flowers, the land would be bare. Also, do not touch flowers or urinate on them. Your body's salts and acids can attract animals that will trample or dig up vegetation. There are ways to enjoy plants without disturbing them: photograph them, sketch them, identify them—but leave them untouched.

The wildlife you encounter on trips should be viewed from a distance and not disturbed. You are only a guest, for these lands are home to these wild animals. Never feed wildlife. We have a saying in Colorado: "A fed bear is a dead bear." This is true for other large mammals as well. If you feed a bear, it will develop a preference for human food and attempt to flip trash cans, break into houses, or raid hikers' packs to get more of it. On its first offense, the bear is ear-tagged by wildlife officials; on its second offense, it is killed. And who is really to blame? Surely not the person who initially fed the bear! If you feed wildlife, you may as well give that animal a death warrant. Animals can forage for themselves. They don't need your help. For more on proper food storage, see page 77.

Chapter 10

BACKPACKING WITH THE FAMILY

When I was young, we camped and hiked as a family. Mostly we camped out of our car or hiked in the local park. But to my brother and me, even that was something new, something fun, and something we were always excited to do.

Today, spending time outdoors gives me more pleasure than anything. It is my livelihood and an eternal source of joy, contemplation, and discovery. I thank my parents for planting the seed, and I would like more than anything to give that gift to my own children someday.

If you are up for an additional backpacking challenge, bringing your children on a trip can be a rewarding experience for all of you. There are many special techniques and precautions when taking your little ones on a wilderness adventure. And taking a baby backpacking is different from taking a toddler.

You must realize that taking a helpless, dependent child into the woods is a big responsibility. At minimum, you need a few backpacking trips under your belt before you take your children along. Once you feel confident using your equipment and dealing with difficult situations like unfavorable weather or poorly defined trails, you are ready to travel with children.

The trip becomes more manageable when you include one or two other adults. If you are carrying a baby on your back, you will need someone else to carry your gear and the baby's gear.

• •

"**M**y most memorable experience was climbing Mt. Rainier when I was twelve. At the time I was the youngest girl to climb Mt. Rainier. I had a female guide; her name was Robin. I was with my dad and a group of eighteen macho rugby players from Rochester, New York. I was the only girl, except for my leader. I vomited from altitude sickness when I reached the summit, and I sunburned the roof of my mouth. My body hurt for days. But I was in better shape than those rugby guys! I was very proud; I wrote my college essay about that experience. Even today I look back and get strength from it. My guide Robin really inspired me. She was tough. I remember wanting to be just like her."

—Jennifer Botzojorns, age 33

• •

With the right gear and the right attitude, children can be excellent backpackers.

Obviously this will be quite a load—one reason why you can count on traveling far fewer miles than you would if you left the kids behind.

The mere suggestion of taking your kids backpacking may make you shudder and think, Not a chance! But most mothers who take their children along don't regret it.

The thrill of seeing a hawk glide over a field, head cocked, talons erect, and swoop to the ground to take a mouse; the thunder of a river cascading 200 feet over moss-covered rocks and churning in the pool below; the smell of honeysuckle and the delicate art of sucking its nectar—these are gifts you can give your child. Paula Rinaldi-Howse agrees wholeheartedly: "For me, the best moment backpacking was realizing that I'd passed on my love of the outdoors to my kids."

Many of the suggestions that I offer for hiking with infants and toddlers are taken from Barbara J. Eusser's book *Take 'Em Along* and from *Kids in the Wild: A Family Guide to Outdoor Recreation* by Cindy Ross and Todd Gladfelter. For these and other good books on the subject, see the "Share the experience" section in the Resource Directory, page 139.

● ●

"**M**y most memorable backpacking moment was reaching
the bridge over the Delaware
River after completing the
whole Appalachian Trail in
Pennsylvania with my three sons,
then ages seven, nine, and
eleven."

—Elizabeth Fox, age 55

● ●
● ●

"**I** prefer six- or seven-day trips
with my husband and thirteen-
year-old twin boys. It gives us
time away from the usual grind.
For me, the best moment backpacking was realizing that I'd
passed on my love of the outdoors
to my kids. They've been backpacking since they were less than
a year old and are totally comfortable in the woods."

—Paula Rinaldi-Howse, age 43

● ●

BEFORE YOU GO

Preparation

When you plan a trip with children, involve them in the planning process. Give them some ownership of the trip. Offer a choice of destinations and let your children make the final decision. Choose a tangible destination like a lake or a shelter that the kids will be excited to get to. Make the destination realistic, and plan on covering few miles. The object is not to wear everyone out (including yourself), but to enjoy the walk and keep the kids interested and comfortable.

You can do additional things to build excitement into the planning stage. Set your tent up in the yard and spend the night in it so your children become comfortable with sleeping outdoors. Have the kids wear their hiking shoes to school. Let them help you prepare food for the trip—and make sure to bring their favorite foods. (Fortunately, children's favorite meals usually include spaghetti, macaroni and cheese, and peanut butter and jelly—all of which are easy to prepare in the wilderness.) Plan a practice run: Hike a mile or two into the woods, spend the night, and hike out. This may be all you'll ever want to tackle. But if you embark on a couple one-night trips and emerge with minimal battle wounds, you can handle a longer trip.

Equipment

Along with your children's clothing and equipment, there are additional items you will want to pack.

Expand your first-aid kit: Bring plenty of Band-Aids and antibiotic ointment, and add items such as butterfly Band-Aids and children's Tylenol for fevers—items you may have considered optional in your own travels. I strongly recommend taking a first-aid course before you take children backpacking. You will feel more confident if you are prepared for the worst case scenario.

Consider carrying a larger tent. Your children may not be thrilled about spending extended periods of time in the confining interior of a tent. If you have an infant, you might need to comfort your baby in the middle of the night. A tent that is large enough to stand up in may be worth the extra weight. If you need to nurse your baby at night, a thick mattress pad will allow you to do so comfortably.

Your children need their own gear. Packs, boots, and sleeping bags must fit children or they'll be miserable. You may be apprehensive about spending money on boots and packs that your children will soon grow out of, but their comfort level will ultimately determine whether your children think about outdoor activities in a positive way or shudder at the thought of leaving home.

Finally, don't forget to bring your flexibility and sense of humor!

Packs

If you're bringing a very small baby along, you'll need a pack designed for carrying her. Most child carriers can hold up to 40 or 60 pounds and cost between $100 and $200. These backpacks have one large space for your child and a small compartment to store diapers, snacks, water, or other items that you may need to access quickly. There typically isn't room for carrying much more. That is why you need to hike with a hardy soul who can sport all your other belongings.

If you are bringing a toddler, he or she should carry a small school backpack with a snack and water, a jacket, and a favorite toy. It is good to get your children accustomed to carrying something and to let them be responsible for an important piece of equipment, such as a flashlight. They should understand that the most important items to carry are those that provide food, drink, and warmth. Also, make sure they carry a whistle for emergencies, and teach them to use a whistle when they are lost or injured. But make sure they understand that the whistle is for emergencies only! Three blows is the signal for distress. Practice first, and give them scenarios and let them tell you if it is an emergency situation.

Child carrier

TRAIL GAMES FOR THE KIDS
. . . .

Entertaining children in the woods may sound like a challenge. If someone gets bored, you won't have a VCR, video games, or books and toys from home to use as a quick fix. But if you're creative you'll find numerous ways to entertain children in the backcountry.

- Sing favorite songs as you walk.
- Learn as you go. "Find Two Animal Signs" (these can be tracks, scat, a bird nest, scratches on a tree, etc.) or "Who Will Be the First to Find a Maple Tree?" (or other specific type of plant, etc.). Younger kids can search for specific colors or numbers of items.
- Play name games. For example, start with "I'm going hiking and I'm going to bring an apple." The next person repeats what you've said and adds their own item that starts with the letter B. Continue through the alphabet.

(continued on page 128)

TRAIL GAMES FOR THE KIDS

• • • • • • • • • • • • • • • •

(continued from page 127)

- Play "I Spy." One person thinks of an object seen on the trail ("I Spy something purple!"), and everyone else asks "yes" or "no" questions until they can guess what the object is. We usually start out by asking "Is it bigger than a shoebox?" and "Is it alive?" This helps narrow it down.

- Bring a small magnifying glass so kids can look at bugs, leaves, etc.

- Bring lightweight toys like balloons or puppets.

- In camp, play family games like charades.

- Bring a favorite book to read before bedtime.

Older children, starting around age seven or eight, can carry more weight. As they get older and approach junior high school, they will need a backpack with a frame to carry their equipment. Children's packs come in both internal and external frame models, and most are considerably less expensive than your own backpack or child carrier. Look for packs that have a lot of adjustments so you can expand the pack to fit your child during growth-spurt years.

Determining the amount of weight children can carry may require some experimentation. Generally, children should not carry more than one-fourth of their body weight. Let older children pack their gear themselves—then make sure a few too many toys didn't find their way into the pack! Give children an equipment checklist to make sure they don't forget an important item. Weigh the loaded pack on a scale to make sure that it is an appropriate weight for your child.

Boots

Sneakers will suffice for a while. But as your child gets older and begins to carry his or her own backpack, hiking shoes become necessary. A comfortable fit is essential or your child will want to be on the first trail out of the woods. Have a salesperson fit your child's foot to a boot, and take time to get the right fit. Sometimes it's difficult for a child to tell if a boot fits or not—especially when the boot looks good and your child just *has* to have it. Boots should be broken in for at least a week or two before the trip. Children's boots range from $20 to over $100. Get the boot that fits best and is the highest quality your budget will allow. Take proper care of the boots, and teach your children how to care for them as well (boot care is covered on page 40).

Sleeping bags

Babies, toddlers, and older children all need their own sleeping area.

A small sleeping pad, lots of clothes, and several baby blankets should keep your baby warm. A full body jumper with feet and a hat is a good outfit for the night.

Older children need a sleeping pad and a sleeping bag. Closed-cell foam sleeping pads are inexpensive; cut the pad to fit your child's body. Fold a child's sleeping bag underneath itself to make the bag the right size for a small child. This will provide extra cushioning and reduce the space the child's body must heat in order to stay warm. If you sew, you may want to make a child-sized sleeping bag. Most children's sleeping bags are not that much smaller than adult bags. When you buy an older child's bag, choose a temperature rating that is lower than the lowest temperature you expect to encounter.

ON THE TRAIL

Make sure your baby is dressed appropriately and has plenty of water. Remember, your baby is sitting still back there; in cooler weather, he or she will need to be dressed much more warmly than you. Check your baby's skin frequently to make sure he or she is not too cold. If your child is a good crawler, take breaks in areas that are void of baby hazards. Scout out the area first and avoid places with nearby cliffs, fast-flowing water, sharp rocks, and cactus.

Safety is important for older children too. In addition to teaching your kids about using whistles to call for help in an emergency, have children wear bright colors so you can spot them easily. Have all members of your group stick together. If older children want to separate from parents, make sure they use the buddy system. Stop for snacks and water frequently so the kids stay energized and hydrated. Check their feet during the day for hot spots or blisters; taking care of minor foot discomforts before they become major problems will make life more enjoyable for all of you. You may also want to have your children wear name tags that list their age, medical needs, phone number, trip itinerary, and campsite. If they become lost, it will be easy for another hiker to return them to their party.

As you hike, show your kids minimum-impact techniques. Teach them to respect the envi-

BABES IN THE WOODS

When you take an infant backpacking:

- Feel your baby's skin periodically to make sure he or she is not too cold.
- Dress your baby in synthetic layers day and night.
- Carry a larger tent to have room to comfort your baby and to nurse comfortably.
- Have your baby sleep in a baby sack (a tiny sleeping bag with legs).
- If your baby can crawl, be aware of natural hazards in the area.
- Air-dry urine-soaked cloth diapers to make them lighter to carry and to reuse the next day.

"**W**hen I was a child and teenager, my parents always took me and my sister on trips in and around mountains. As a fourteen-year-old, I hiked Mt. Washington and stayed on the summit in the old Yankee building. This was one of the most memorable experiences of my life."

—Laurie Gordon, age 37

CHILDREN AND ANIMALS

• • • • • • • • • • • • • • • •

It is important to let children experience nature by touching and watching and exploring. Encourage children to have fun, but make sure you instill in them an attitude of respect. Here are a few things to tell them before hitting the trail.

- You are a visitor in the animals' home. Behave as you would if you went over to a friend's house. Respect their home.
- Keep your distance from animals, even ones that might look friendly.
- Certain animals can be dangerous. (Be specific about the animals in the area you're traveling.)
- Don't torture animals, especially insects.
- Do not feed animals; they need to know how to get food for themselves.

ronment. Don't let them race through springs that serve as drinking holes, stomp on fragile vegetation, scare or hurt animals, or make loud noises at crowded campsites.

When you bring a baby, you will have to pack out used diapers. You may want to bring cloth diapers, since they are light and compact and can be reused. Plan on carrying a large supply since it's quite difficult to wash them on the trail. Never wash diapers in a stream, in a lake, or in any other water source. Instead, turn a Ziploc bag into a washing machine and then discard the dirty water far from any water source.

Be flexible about the number of miles you travel in a day. Develop a Plan B, in case your troop doesn't feel up to the mileage you had in mind. If your kids are sluggish, call it a day.

When you get to camp, older children should be responsible for certain camp chores. It is good for them to take responsibility for the trip, and you can use the help with pitching the tent, organizing gear, collecting water, and cooking. In the morning, plan on taking considerably longer to pack your gear and get on the trail.

Taking the family backpacking is no easy task. But it can certainly be made more manageable if you are prepared and flexible. It is something that your little ones will appreciate for a lifetime.

Chapter 11

PLANNING LONGER TRIPS

During the past century, wildlands have vanished at an astonishing rate. I for one am thankful that during the transformation of natural areas into urban, agricultural, and industrial areas, some people had the foresight to preserve tracts of land that link the wilderness. Continuous footpaths that span vast regions, even entire continents, should be hiked and cherished—simply because they exist in a world where wilderness is becoming endangered.

To walk a long-distance trail is to develop a bond with the land and the people who inhabit it. It is the best way I've found to see a country or explore a region. And it is, truly, a delightful way to live.

GETTING STARTED

Long-distance hikes involve traveling along trails for extended periods of time, generally for a month or longer. Because you cannot carry food and supplies such long distances, you must arrange to have packages sent to post offices along the way. You will typically experience a variety of weather conditions. And you will become accustomed to hiking and camping as a way of life, as Susan-Gail Arey has: ". . . in March 1976, I started the Appalachian Trail. I learned to backpack just so I could hike the trail. I figured this hike would be my only trip. In fact, a lot of

• •

"**O**ne day in 1965, my best friend came home from a trip and told us she'd heard of a trail 2,000 miles long. We started making plans for it and talking about how we would do it. We didn't even know there was a thing called backpacking. We thought you had to carry food for the whole 2,000 miles. After several months, the others lost interest—but the idea just wouldn't let me go, and I knew someday I had to do it.

"One thing that held me up was that I didn't know how to get started and I didn't have anyone to go with. But one night in December 1974, I decided to find out how to backpack and hike the trail alone. I still didn't know if you had to carry your food for 2,000 miles.

"Then in March 1976, I started the Appalachian Trail. I learned to backpack just so I could hike the trail. I figured this hike would be my only trip. In fact, a lot of the time that first week I swore I'd never backpack again, and I wished I had never heard of the trail. It was cold, rainy, and steep. But things changed, the weather improved, and I got stronger. By the time I finished in October 1976, I knew I could not tell this delightful way of life good-bye."

—Susan-Gail Arey, age 44

• •

the time that first week I swore I'd never backpack again, and I wished I had never heard of the trail. It was cold, rainy, and steep. But things changed, the weather improved, and I got stronger. By the time I finished in October 1976, I knew I could not tell this delightful way of life good-bye."

Being a long-distance hiker is a healthy, invigorating, and challenging way to live—and it is something anyone can do. You don't need to be an expert; you just need to be familiar with your equipment and your abilities, plan ahead, and be very determined. When I began my Appalachian Trail hike, I was shocked to hear about so many people on the trail who had little to no experience backpacking. Practice is truly the best way to learn.

If you think you may be interested in planning a long-distance hike, there are a few steps you should take to get started. First, determine how much time you have to hike a long trail. I found that the majority of long-distance backpackers just graduated from high school or college, or they are retired. A few quit their jobs to hike. Almost no one leaves children they are raising. For most people, finding a substantial amount of time for backpacking is quite difficult.

As you consider your time frame, also consider what seasons are best for particular parts of the country. For example, if you want to hike the Appalachian Trail, you must recognize that snow prevents access to the northern terminus in Maine between November and May. So if you start from the south, you need to plan on finishing before November; if you start from the north, you may not be able to begin hiking until June.

As you're thinking about a time frame, you should also be thinking about a specific trail. There are a number of National Scenic Trails and National Historic Trails that are federally designated and protected. For contact information for specific trails, see the Resource Directory.

National Scenic Trails

- Appalachian Trail: 2,150 miles, Georgia to Maine

- Continental Divide Trail: 3,200 miles, Mexican border to Canadian border

- Florida Trail: 1,300 miles, Big Cypress National Preserve to western panhandle

- Ice Age Trail: 1,000 miles, Lake Michigan to Saint Croix River

- Natchez Trace Trail: 110 miles, Natchez, Mississippi, to Nashville, Tennessee

- North Country Trail: 3,200 miles, Adirondack Mountains, New York, to Missouri River in South Dakota

- Pacific Crest Trail: 2,600 miles, Mexican border to Canadian border

- Potomac Heritage Trail: 700 miles, Virginia, Maryland, District of Columbia, Pennsylvania

The "big three" long trails are the Appalachian Trail (AT), the Pacific Crest Trail (PCT), and the Continental Divide Trail (CDT). Of these, the most popular and well traveled is the AT. It is the easiest trail to follow, the easiest to resupply during, and arguably the most challenging and most monotonous terrain. By contrast, the PCT crosses a diverse range of environments, from desert to alpine tundra, and it is becoming increasingly more popular. The CDT is not well defined. In fact it does not exist at all in many places, and you must be proficient with a map and compass to hike it. The Continental Divide Trail Alliance is hoping to complete the trail and publish guide books within the next ten years.

There are a handful of other long-distance trails that are equally spectacular, but they do not bear the Congress-designated status of a National Trail. Other popular long-distance trails include the Long Trail (Vermont), the Colorado Trail, the John Muir Trail (California), and the recently established American Discovery Trail that traverses the continent in an east-to-west direction and goes through urban and rural areas.

For other ideas about long-distance trails, take a look at Charles Cook's *The Essential Guide to Hiking in the U.S.* (see the "Where to go" section of the Resource Directory, page 139), peruse the book department at your local outfitting store, or ask local trail clubs for ideas.

Once you decide on a trail, contact the trail's headquarters for more information (addresses are listed in the Resource Directory, page 137). Many long-distance trails have handbooks and guidebooks to assist you on your journey; selected titles are listed

Long-distance hikers along the Pacific Crest Trail, Washington. (Photo by Eric Sanford/Mountain Stock)

in the Resource Directory. These publications will give you addresses for post offices along the way, help you plan your food drops and what equipment to bring, give you an idea about the terrain and trail conditions, and discuss mileage, campsites, water sources, and towns along the way.

If you like the idea of long-distance hiking, but taking a year off work is out of the question, consider hiking parts of long trails. Most people do not attempt a continuous hike of a 2,000-mile trail. Instead, many are section hikers, trekking a few weeks or a month at a time. This is an excellent way to get a feel for the long-distance hiker's life and still maintain your normal life and responsibilities. You can also be more selective in the part of the trail you choose to hike. Pick a highlight of a long-distance trail or a region you've always wanted to see. Some hikers piece together long-distance trails on day hikes or week-long hikes. For some, it is a goal and an obsession, and it may take them ten, twenty, even thirty years to complete the trail.

FOOD AND SUPPLIES

Your care packages, or mail drops, require meticulous planning. Use your guidebooks to determine how many miles you need to travel before you can resupply—that is, before you can hike to town or catch a ride there to pick up your mail. Then decide how long it will take you to walk that many miles.

If you must travel 45 miles to the next town and you plan on hiking about 10 miles a day, then you should carry food for five days. On the fifth day, hike five miles, then get your resupply box. In your box you should have food for the number of days it will take you to get to the next mail drop.

If you are hiking a long-distance trail, planning your menu for six months or so can be difficult. I usually break it down into the number of breakfasts, lunches, and dinners I'll need per box. It is important to put plenty of snacks in each box. It is better to have a little too much food than to run out. If you realize you've sent yourself too much food, you can always send it home or send it ahead to supplement another mail drop.

It is also critical to vary your meals. Don't plan on eating oatmeal for every breakfast and pasta for every dinner—you will soon dread each mail drop! Put a treat in every box so you have something to look forward to. You can include a favorite snack that may be too heavy to carry but can be consumed before you leave town.

In addition to food, fill your supply boxes with fresh underwear, socks, and a T-shirt as well as clothes to match changing weather conditions. For example, if you are hiking into autumn, your box might contain warmer clothes for when the temperatures drop.

Your guidebooks will have suggestions for items relevant to your trail. Some ideas for restocking your equipment include: extra batteries; Band-Aids, moleskin, or other items that you may have used from your first-aid kit; new boot laces; iodine tablets or a replacement filter for your water purifier; film; vitamins; sunscreen; a new book, extra paper, envelopes and stamps; traveler's checks; guidebooks for the upcoming section of trail.

Pack and address the boxes before you leave and have a trusted friend or family member send each box as you move along the trail. Do not seal the boxes until they are ready to be mailed. That way you can have your friend include extra items as you need them. If the weather is warmer than you expected, have your friend add a tank top to your next box instead of waiting three weeks for the warm-weather clothes box to arrive. It's not necessary to arrange for post office boxes; simply send the packages to yourself, marked "General Delivery." Some post offices will hold mail for only a limited time, so make sure your boxes don't arrive months before you do.

Plan to receive mail drops in towns that are accessible to the trail and that have other conveniences. You may need to buy extra food, visit a pharmacy, or buy fuel for your stove. Since you cannot mail fuel, you need to visit towns where the right type of fuel is available. Timing is also important. Arriving in town on Saturday afternoon or Sunday is unfortunate because you'll have to wait until Monday for the post office and stores to open. Unless you're on a tight schedule, this may be a good excuse to take a break. You no doubt will find things to do: sleep, eat nondehydrated food, write, and clean up. Arriving in town at the "right" time takes more luck than planning, since you will seldom be able to stick to your original schedule. You may want to travel more miles one day, take a day off at a lake, or take a side trip. As a long-distance hiker, you learn to roll with whatever comes up. Somehow, things tend to work out.

FINAL WORDS

Long-distance trails are often more of a mental challenge than a physical one. You need to know when to take a break. I've learned from experience that you want to enjoy the walk—not just fin-

• •

"I prefer extended trips. For me, it is the lifestyle of through-hiking. Reducing your needs to food, shelter, and water in a world full of sensory overload is very appealing."

—Leticia Lacativa, age 35

• •

ish it. When hiking starts to be more work than fun, take a day off and evaluate your situation. Everyone has her own idea of what long-distance hiking should be, and you need to hike the hike that is right for you. There is no wrong way to do it, as long as you're having fun. The generosity of strangers, the self-sufficient lifestyle, the feeling of accomplishment, the way you feel yourself evolving: These are the memories you will create if you're doing it right.

A detailed discussion of every aspect of long distance hiking is beyond the scope of this book, but I hope you get an idea of how far you can take the sport of backpacking. It is something to tuck away in the back of your mind as you take your first few trips into the wilderness. Imagine what it would be like to live like that for months instead of days.

Chapter 12

🥾 RESOURCE DIRECTORY

There are many advantages to traveling with a partner or with a group. Generally, people feel more secure in the wilderness if there are others around to decipher unfamiliar sounds at night, locate a camp site, or assist in an emergency. Group travel also allows each member to carry less weight since gear and food can be shared. For me, the greatest benefit of backpacking with other women is sharing the experience. The bond between women seems to be enhanced on backpacking trips; wilderness has a way of bringing people together.

Chances are you already know women who backpack. Women's involvement in backpacking and in most outdoor activities has increased dramatically during the past decade. However, if you don't know anyone who backpacks or if you're looking for new companions with interests similar to your own, you may want to tap into a network of outdoor organizations and connect with other backpacking women. National organizations The American Hiking Society and the Sierra Club have local chapters in most states. Long-distance trail organizations usually have local hiking clubs and trail maintenance clubs in the states through which the trails pass. Often, outdoors-outfitting stores sponsor hikes and can help you locate hiking or outdoor clubs in your area. Your local outfitter or chamber of commerce may be able to give you more information about local trail maintenance groups and conservation societies.

Volunteering for trail maintenance is an excellent way to meet people with common interests and to give something back to the trails and wildlands. Government funding for trail systems has always been low, so outdoors enthusiasts rely on each other to build and maintain trails. Contact your state's Parks and Recreation Department, the Appalachian Trail Conference, the Pacific Crest Trail, The Colorado Trail, or the Continental Divide Trail for information about volunteer opportunities and local chapters.

When you contact someone who is interested in going backpacking, it is a good idea to meet for lunch or go for a walk before you plan a trip together. This person may be a friend of a friend, a casual acquaintance, or a complete stranger. You need to make sure you both have the same goals for the trip. You need to be able to completely trust one another to act responsibly in an emergency situation, bring appropriate and functional gear, and be a team player. It could be disastrous if your companion races ahead with your tent and dinner and assumes you'll catch up by the end of the day. Get to know your partner and her abilities, experience level, and goals. Go for a day hike together before you set out on an overnight trip.

What follows is a compilation of resources for the backpacker at any level. It begins with a list of books mentioned in the text, as well as books that have been useful or inspiring to me over the years. Subjects include inspiring tales of women adventurers, backcountry cooking, gear selection and maintenance, using map and compass, low-impact techniques, desert and alpine backpacking, wilderness first-aid, and hiking with children.

The next section provides a plethora of backpacking organizations and other ways to connect with adventurous women all over the world. Included there is information about women's courses and travel, national and regional hiking organizations, long-distance trail conferences, and outdoor organizations state by state so you can locate the ones nearest you.

It is time. It is time to get out there, to connect with other women, to apply what you've learned about backpacking, to share your knowledge and learn from others. I wish you the merriest of travels, the sunniest days, the most spectacular views, the most fulfilling adventures. Explore, think, connect, challenge yourself, and most of all, have fun.

Books

GET IN THE MOOD

Blum, Arlene. *Annapurna: A Woman's Place*. San Francisco: Sierra Club Books, 1983.

Fagg Olds, Elizabeth. *Women of the Four Winds: The Adventures of Four of America's First Women Explorers*. Boston: Houghton Mifflin Company, 1985.

LaBastille, Anne. *Women and Wilderness*. San Francisco, Sierra Club Books, 1984.

Mazel, David, ed. *Mountaineering Women: Stories by Early Climbers*. College Station, TX: Texas A&M University Press, 1997.

FUEL UP

Barker, Harriet. *The One-Burner Gourmet*. Chicago: Contemporary Books, 1981.

Fleming, June. *The Well-Fed Backpacker*. New York: Vintage Books, 1986.

Kesselheim, Alan S. *Trail Food: Drying and Cooking Food for Backpackers and Paddlers*. Camden, ME: Ragged Mountain Press, 1998.

McHugh, Gretchen. *The Hungry Hiker's Book of Good Cooking*. New York: Alfred K. Knopf, 1996.

Miller, Dorcas S. *Good Food for Camp and Trail: All-Natural Recipes for Delicious Meals Outdoors*. Boulder, CO: Pruett, 1993.

GEAR UP

Getchell, Annie. *The Essential Outdoor Gear Manual:*

Equipment Care & Repair for Outdoorspeople. Camden, ME: Ragged Mountain Press, 1995.

Sumner, Louise Lindgren. *Sew and Repair Your Outdoor Gear.* Seattle, WA: The Mountaineers, 1988.

GET GOING—AND GET BACK

Curtis, Rick. *The Backpacker's Field Manual: A Comprehensive Guide to Mastering Backcountry Skills.* Pittsburgh, PA: Three Rivers Press, 1998.

Fleming, June. *Staying Found: The Complete Map & Compass Handbook.* Seattle: The Mountaineers, 1994.

Geary, Don. *Using a Map and Compass.* Mechanicsburg, PA: Stackpole Books, 1995.

Kellstrom, Bjorn. *Be Expert With Map and Compass: The Complete Orienteering Handbook.* New York: Macmillan, 1994.

Seidman, David. *The Essential Wilderness Navigator.* Camden, ME: Ragged Mountain Press, 1995.

GO LIGHTLY

Cole, David N. *Low-Impact Recreational Practices for Wilderness and Backcountry.* Gen. Tech. Rep. INT-265. Ogden, UT: U.S. Department of Agriculture, Forest Service, Intermountain Research Station, 1989.

Harmon, Will. *Leave No Trace: Minimum Impact Outdoor Recreation.* Helena, MT: Falcon Press, 1997.

Hampton, Bruce and David Cole. *How to Enjoy the Wilderness Without Harming It.* Mechanicsburg, PA: Stackpole Books, 1995.

McGivney, Annette. *Backpacker's Leave No Trace: A Practical Guide to the New Wilderness Ethic.* Seattle,WA: The Mountaineers, 1998.

WHERE TO GO

Bruce, Dan "Wingfoot." *The Thru-Hiker's Handbook: A Guide for End-to-End Hikes of the Appalachian Trail.* Conyers, GA: Center for Appalachian Trail Studies published yearly).

Cook, Charles. *The Essential Guide to Hiking in the U.S.: All Major Trails and Hiking Areas including National and State Parks, Forests and Preserves.* New York: Michael Kesend Publishing, 1992.

Dudley, Ellen and Eric Seaborg. *American Discoveries: Scouting the First Coast-to-Coast Recreational Trail.* Seattle, WA: The Mountaineers, 1996.

Jacobs, Randy. *The Colorado Trail: The Official Guidebook.* Photography by John Fielder. Englewood, CO: Westcliffe Publishers, Inc. 1994.

Jardine, Ray. *The Pacific Crest Trail Hiker's Handbook: Innovative Techniques and Trail Tested Instruction for the Long-Distance Hiker.* LaPine, OR: AdventureLore Press, 1996.

Schaffer, Jeffrey, P., et al. *The Pacific Crest Trail, Vol.1: California,* 5th ed. Berkeley: Wilderness Press, 1995.

Schaffer, Jeffrey P. and Andy Selters. *The Pacific Crest Trail, Vol. 2: Oregon and Washington,* 5th ed. Berkeley: Wilderness Press, 1990.

Starr, Walter A., Jr. *Starr's Guide to the John Muir Trail and the High Sierra Region,* 12th revised ed. San Francisco: Sierra Club Books, 1982.

GO FARTHER

Conover, Garrett and Alexandra Conover. *A Snow Walker's Companion: Winter Trail Skills from the Far North.* Camden, ME: Ragged Mountain Press, 1995.

Gabbard, Andrea. *Mountaineering: A Woman's Guide.* Camden, ME: Ragged Mountain Press, 1998.

Ganci, Dave. *Desert Hiking.*

Berkeley: Wilderness Press, 1993.

Gorman, Stephen. *AMC Guide to Winter Camping.* Boston, MA: AMC Books, 1991

Mueser, Roland. *Long-Distance Hiking: Lessons from the Appalachian Trail.* Camden, ME: Ragged Mountain Press, 1998.

Townsend, Chris. *Wilderness Skiing and Winter Camping.* Camden, ME: Ragged Mountain Press, 1994.

GO SAFELY

Armstrong, Betsy R. and Knox Williams. *Avalanche Book.* Golden, CO: Fulcrum Publishing, 1992.

Breyfogle, Newell D. *Commonsense Outdoor Medicine.* 3rd edition. Camden, ME: Ragged Mountain Press, 1993.

Darvill, Fred T. *Mountaineering Medicine: A Wilderness Medicine Guide.* 13th revised ed. Berkeley, CA: Wilderness Press, 1992.

Gill, Paul G., Jr., M.D. *The Ragged Mountain Press Pocket Guide to Wilderness Medicine and First-Aid.* Camden, ME: Ragged Mountain Press, 1997.

Schimelpfenig, Tod and Linda Lindsey. *NOLS Wilderness First-Aid.* Mechanicsburg, PA: Stackpole Books, 1992.

Wilkerson, James A., ed. *Medicine for Mountaineering & Other Wilderness Activities.* 4th ed. Seattle, WA: The Mountaineers, 1992.

SHARE THE EXPERIENCE

Euser, Barbara J. *Take 'Em Along: Sharing the Wilderness with Your Children.* Boulder, CO: Johnson Books, 1987.

Liston, Beverly. *Family Camping Made Simple: Tent and RV Camping with Children.* Chester, CT: The Globe Pequot Press, 1989.

Ross, Cindy and Todd Gladfelter. *Kids in the Wild: A Family Guide to Outdoor Recreation.* Seattle, WA: The Mountaineers, 1995.

Silverman, Goldie. *Backpacking with Babies and Small Children*. Berkeley, CA: Wilderness Press, 1986.

Magazines and Websites

Adventure West
http://www.adventurewest.com

American Park Network
Publisher of award-winning visitor guide magazines for national parks, state parks, and wildlife parks.
100 Pine Street, Suite 2850
San Francisco, CA 94111
Phone 415-788-2228
email: apn@sfo.com
http://www.americanparknetwork.com

Backpacker Magazine
Subscriptions
PO Box 7590
Red Oak, IA 51591
Phone 800-666-3434, 515-242-0287
Fax 712-623-5731
email: backpackdm@aol.com
http://www.bpbasecamp.com
Women's page at http://www.bpbase-camp.com/womenspage
Hiking partner wanted postings at http://www.bpbasecamp.com/trail_talk

The Backpacker
Has an interesting question-and-answer page. Maintained by Flycast Communications.
Flycast Communications Corporation
181 Fremont Street
San Francisco, CA 94105
Phone 415-977-1000
Fax 415-977-1009
email: matt@thebackpacker.com
http://www.thebackpacker.com

Backpacker's Guide to the Internet
Reference guide to resources on the web for budget travelers.
http://www.geocities.com/Yosemite/6241/backpackers_guide.htm

Backpacking in America
A photographic exploration of beautiful wilderness areas in the United States; includes backpacking forums.

http://www.chicweb.com/domain/dnl/Backpacking.html

Blue
"A journal for the new traveler."
Subscriptions
PO Box 3000
Denville, NJ 07834
Phone 212-777-0024
Fax 212-777-0068
email: editorial@bluemagazine.com
http://www.bluemagazine.com

Condè Nast Sports for Women
Subscriptions
PO Box 50033
Boulder, CO 80322
Phone 800-274-0084
http://www.condenet.com/subscriptions/sports.html

European Long-Distance Footpaths
Presented by the European Ramblers Association, information about hiking paths criss-crossing many countries.
email: epaths@bibloset.demon.co.uk
http://www.gorp.com/gorp/activity/europe/Epaths.htm

Explore
PO Box 17276
Boulder, CO 80308
Phone 303-413-0338
Fax 303-449-7805
email: info@ExploreOnline.com
http://www.exploremag.com

Get Lost Adventure Magazine
http://www.itsnet.com/home/getlost/mag.html

GORP: Great Outdoors Recreation Pages
http://www.gorp.com

GreatOutdoors
611 South Congress Avenue, Suite 350
Austin, TX 78704
Phone 512-416-5035
Fax 512-707-0181
email: info@greatoutdoors.com
http://www.greatoutdoors.com

The Mountain Zone
911 Western Avenue, Suite 302
Seattle, WA 98104
Phone 206-621-8630

Fax 206-621-0651
email: info@mountainzone.com
http://www.mountainzone.com

National Geographic Traveler
http://www.nationalgeographic.com/media/traveler

Outside Magazine
Subscriptions
PO Box 54729
Boulder, CO 80322
Phone 800-678-1131, 505-989-7100
email: contact.outside@starwave.com
http://outside.starwave.com

Views from the Top
"The premier hiking and climbing webzine"
http://www.lexicomm.com/views/index.html

Wilderness Education Council of Washington
email: bwakeley@aol.com
http://www.washington.edu/trails/wedc/index.html

W.I.G. (Women in General)
PO Box 158
Heber City, UT 84032
Phone 801-654-5398
Fax 801-654-5881
email: wigmag@aol.com
http://www.wigmag.com

Shop for Gear by Mail and Online

Adventure Gear
125 Deer Forest Road
Fayetteville, GA 30214
Phone 888-241-1864
    770-460-9893
Fax 770-460-6693
email: adventure@ewalker.com
http://www.ewalker.com

Adventure Guide Inc.
392 King Street North
Waterloo, Ontario
Canada N0J 1B0
Phone 519-886-3121
Fax 519-886-8179
email: wmaster@advguide.com
http://www.advguide.com

Arizona Hikingshack
11649 North Cave Creek Road
Phoenix, AZ 85020
Phone 800-964-1673
Fax 602-861-0221
email: paul@hikingshack.com
http://www.hikingshack.com

Base Camp Wilderness Outfitters
Phone 888-982-9707
email: support@basecamper.com
http://www.basecamper.com

Brigade Quartermasters
Action Gear
Kennesaw, GA
Phone 770-428-6870, 770-428-1248
email: brigade@brigade.com
http://www.actiongear.com

Cabela's
One Cabela Drive
Sidney, NE 69160
TelPhone 800-237-4444
Fax 800-496-6329
http://www.cabelas.com

CampCo
3311 La Cienega Place
Los Angeles, CA 90016
Phone 310-815-2929
Fax 310-836-5306
email: campco@primenet.com
http://www.campco.com

Campmor
PO Box 700-M
Upper Saddle River, NJ 07458
Phone 800-CAMPMOR
Fax 800-230-2153
customer-service@campmor.com
http://www.campmor.com

Denali Outdoor Recreation
1140 East Brickyard Road
Salt Lake City, UT 84106
Phone 888-4DENALI
801-484-5044
Fax 801-467-5289
email: info@denali1.com
http://www.denali1.com

Edelweiss
08011 Barcelona, Spain
email: consultas@
  som-edelweiss.com
http://www.som-edelweiss.com

L.L. Bean
Freeport, ME 04033-0001
Phone 800-341-4341
Fax 207-552-3080
email: llbean@llbean.com
http://www.llbean.com

REI
Sumner, WA 98352
Phone 800-426-4840
Fax 253-891-2523
Email: service@rei.com
http://www.rei.com

Rocky Mountain Outfitters
1738 Pearl Street
Boulder, CO 80302
http://omix.com/rmo

Totally Outdoors: The Outdoor
Woman's Outfitter
1818 South Quebec Way 12-9
Denver, CO 80231
Fax 800-596-2243
email:
  toutdoors@totallyoutdoors.com
http://www.totallyoutdoors.com

Wildware Outfitters
Phone 800-568-8008
Fax 717-564-1969
email: wildware@igateway.com
http://www.wildware.com

Yucca Dune
Junction of Highways 20 and 83
Valentine, NE 69201
Phone 402-376-3330
Fax 402-376-3330
email: ryschon@ibm.net
http://www.yuccadune.com

Zanika Women's Sportswear
PO Box 119-43
Minneapolis, MN 55411
Phone 612-529-1785
Fax 612-521-4481
email: zanika@ool.com
http://www.halcyon.com/ool/ool/
  zanika.html

Map Resources

DeLorme
2 DeLorme Drive
PO Box 298
Yarmouth, ME 04096
Phone 207-846-7000
Automated product information:
  207-846-7058
email: info@delorme.com
http://www.delorme.com

Earthwalk Press
2239 Union Street
Eureka, CA 95501

Green Trail Maps
PO Box 77734
Seattle, WA 98177
206-546-MAPS
Fax 206-542-0196
email: gtrails@aol.com
http://eskimo.com/~dirkman/
  home.htm

Latitude 40°
303-258-7909

National Park Service
Office of Public Inquiries
1849 C Street NW
Washington, DC 20013
Phone 202-208-6843
http://www.nps.gov

Points West Map & Guidebook
Outfitters
PO Box 2157
Florissant, MO 63032
888-320-9378
email:
  webmasters@pointswestoutfitters.com
http://pointswestoutfitters.com

Tom Harrison Cartography
2 Falmouth Cove
San Rafael, CA 94901
800-265-9090
http://www.tomharrisonmaps.com

Trails Illustrated
PO Box 4357
Evergreen, CO 80437-4357
Phone 800-962-1643
Fax 800-626-8676
email: topomaps@aol.com/trails
http://www.trailsillustrated.com

U.S.D.A. Forest Service
Public Affairs Office
PO Box 96090
Washington, DC 20090-6090
Phone 202-205-1760
Fax 202-205-0885
email: oc/wo@fs.fed.us
http://www.fs.fed.us

U.S. Geological Survey National Center
12201 Sunrise Valley Drive
Reston, VA 20192
Phone 703-648-4000
Fax 703-648-4250
http://www.usgs.gov

Wilderness Press
2440 Bancroft Way
Berkeley, CA 94704
Phone 800-443-7227, 510-843-8080
Fax 510-548-1355
email: wpress@wildernesspress.com
http://www.wildernesspress.com

Travel, Events, and Outdoor Courses

FOR WOMEN

Becoming an Outdoors-Woman
Dr. Christine Thomas
College of Naural Resources
University of Wisconsin–Stevens Point
Stevens Point, WI 54481
http://www.state.nj.us/dep/fgw/bowhome.htm

EarthWise Journeys
A woman-owned company specializing in women's trips that are run by responsible tour operators and outfitters. Features backpacking and trekking trips in the U.S., Canada, Europe, Latin America, and elsewhere.
PO Box 16177
Portland, Oregon, 97292
Phone 503-736-3364
email: earthwyz@teleport.com
http://www.teleport.com/~earthwyz/women.htm

Women in the Wilderness
Washington Outfitters & Guides Association
704 228th Avenue NE
Redmond, WA 98053
Phone 425-392-6107
Fax 425-392-0111
email: Debbyhorse@aol.com
http://www2.ool.com/women/wwwboard/messages/198.shtml

Women's Outdoor Network
PO Box 50003
Palo Alto, CA 94303
Phone 650-494-8583
Fax 650-712-9093
email: wonforfun@earthlink.net
http://home.earthlink.net/~wonforfun/

Women's Sports Foundation
Eisenhower Park
East Meadow, NY 11554
Phone 800-227-3988, 516-542-4700
Fax 516-542-4716
email: wosport@aol.com
http://www.lifetimetv.com/WoSport

GENERAL

Elderhostel
75 Federal Street
Boston, MA 02110
Phone 617-426-8056
email: catalogs@elderhostel.org
http://www.elderhostel.org

National Outdoor Leadership School
288 Main Street
Lander, WY 82520
Phone 307-332-47846973
Phone for Leave No Trace:
800-332-4100
Fax 307-332-1220
email: admissions@nols.edu
http://www.nols.edu/

Outward Bound
National Office
Route 9D
R2 Box 280
Garrison, NY 10524-9757
Phone 800-243-8520
Fax 914-424-4000
http://www.outwardbound.org

Tread Lightly
298 24th Street, Suite 325
Ogden, UT 84401
Phone 800-966-9900
Fax 801-621-8633
http://www.treadlightly.org

Women's Wellness

The Melpomene Institute
1010 University Avenue
St. Paul, MN 55104
Phone 612-642-1951
Fax 612-642-1871
email: melpomen@skypoint.com
http://www.melpomene.org

National and Regional Organizations

American Discovery Trail Society
PO Box 20155
Washington, DC 20041-2155
Phone 800-663-2387
703-753-0149
Fax 703-754-9008
email: adtsociety@aol.com
http://www1.discoverytrail.org/discoverytrail/

American Hiking Society
PO Box 20160
Washington, DC 20009
Phone 301-565-6704
Fax 301-565-6714
email: ahsmmbrshp@aol.com
http://www.lorca.org/ahs

American Trails
PO Box 11046
Prescott, AZ 86304
Phone 520-632-1140
Fax 520-632-1147
email: AmTrails@lankaster.com
http://www.outdoorlink.com/amtrails/

American Volkssport Association
1001 Pat Booker Road Suite 101
Universal City, TX 78148
Phone 800-830-WALK, 210-659-2112
Fax 210-659-1212
email: avahq@juno.com
http://www.ava.org/index.htm

**Appalachian Long-Distance
  Hikers Association**
Benning Street
West Lebanon, NH 03784
email: aldha@connix.com
http://sports.friendfinder.com/
  ffsports/sportsvote/site/urls/157view.
  html

Appalachian Mountain Club
5 Joy Street
Boston, MA 02108
Phone 617-523-0636
Fax 617-523-0722
email: information@amcinfo.org
http://www.outdoors.org

Appalachian Trail Home Page
http://www.fred.net/kathy/at.html

National Park Service
1849 C Street NW
Washington, DC 20240
Phone 202-208-6843
http://www.nps.gov

National Wildlife Federation
8925 Leesburg Pike
Vienna, VA 22184
Phone 800-822-9919, 703-790-4000
http://www.nwf.org

The Nature Conservancy
1815 North Lynn Streert
Arlington, VA 22209
Phone 800-628-6860, 703-841-5300
http://www.tnc.org

The Sierra Club
Second Street, Second Floor
San Francisco, CA 941095
Phone 415-977-5500
Fax 415-977-5799
information@sierraclub.org
http://sierraclub.org

U.S.D.A. Forest Service
PO Box 96090
Washington, DC 20090
Phone 202-205-1760
Fax 202-205-0885 DG: PAO:W01B
email: oc/wo@fs.fed.us
http://www.fs.fed.us

Long-Distance Trail Conferences

Appalachian Trail Conference
PO Box 807
Harpers Ferry, WV 25425
Phone 304-535-6331
email: info@atconf.org
http://www.atconf.org

Colorado Trail Foundation
PO Box 260876
Lakewood, CO 80226
Phone 303-526-0809
http://www.coloradotrail.org

Continental Divide Trail Society
North Charles Street #601
Baltimore, MD 21218
Phone 410-235-9610
email: cdtsociety@aol.com
http://www.gorp.com

Continental Divide Trail Alliance
PO Box 628
Pine, CO 80470
Phone 303-838-3760
Fax 303-838-3960
email: cdnst@aol.com
http://www.cdtrail.org

Florida Trail Association
PO Box 13708
Gainesville, FL 32604
Phone 800-343-1882, 904-378-8823
email: fta@florida-trail.org
http://www.atlantic.net/~fta

Ice Age Park and Trail Foundation
PO Box 423
Pewaukee, WI 53072
Phone 414-691-2776
email: iat@execpc.com
http://www.execpc.com/~iat/
  iceage.htm

Natchez Trace Trail Conference
PO Box 1236
Jackson, MS 39152215
Phone 601-956-0045
email: jhodonttc@aol.com

North Country Trail Association
49 Monroe Center, Suite 200B
Grand Rapids, MI 4954603
Phone 616-454-5506
Fax 616-454-7139
email: NCTAssoc@aol.com
http://people.delphi.com/wesboyd/
  ncnst.htm

Pacific Crest Trail Association
5325 Elkhorn Boulevard, Suite 256
Sacramento, CA 95842
Phone 888-PC-TRAIL,
  916-349-2109
email: pctrail@compuserve.com
http://www.gorp.com/pcta

Potomac Heritage Trail Association
5229 Benson Avenue
Baltimore, MD 21227

State and Local Organizations

The following is a list of organizations listed by state. The organizations may be hiking and outing clubs, trail maintenance and volunteer organizations, or conservation and preservation societies.

ALABAMA

Alabama Department of Economic and Community Affairs
PO Box 5690
401 Adams Avenue
Montgomery, AL 36103
334-242-5483

Alabama Trails Association
PO Box 371162
Birmingham, AL 35237-1162

Lower Appalachian Mountain Club
PO Box 380621
Birmingham, AL 35238
205-991-7609
Fax 205-995-1159
email: alamc@aol.com

Sierra Club—Alabama Chapter
PO Box 2862
Tuscaloosa, AL 35403
205-333-9153
email: peggie.griffin@sierraclub.org
http://www.sierraclub.org/chapters/al

ALASKA

Alaska Backcountry Outfitters
PO Box 491
210 Main Street
Haines, AK 99827
907-766-2876
Fax 907-766-2844
email: aknature@kcd.com
http://kcd.com/aknature

Challenge Alaska
1132 East 74th Avenue, Suite 107
Anchorage, AK 99518
907-344-7399
Fax 907-344-7349
email:
    challenge@arctic.net

Iditarod Trail Blazers
PO Box 1923
Seward, AK 99644

Kachemak Heritage Land Trust
PO Box 2400
Homer, AK 99603
907-235-5263
http://www.xyz.net/~khltkbr

Trail Mix, Inc.
PO Box 211414
Auke Bay, AK 99821-1414
907-790-6406
Fax 907-789-3118
email: trailmix@alaska.net

ARIZONA

Arizona State Parks
1300 West Washington
Phoenix, AZ 85007
800-285-3703
602-542-4174

Arizona Trail Association
PO Box 36736
Phoenix, AZ 85067
602-252-4795
Fax 602-952-1447
email: aztrail@aztrail.org
http://www.primenet.com/aztrail

Huachuca Hiking Club
PO Box 3555
Sierra Vista, AZ 85636-3555

Pima Trails Association
PO Box 41358
Tucson, AZ 85717
520-577-7919

Red Rock Pathways
50 Yucca Street
Sedona, AZ 86351

Sierra Club—Grand Canyon Chapter
516 East Portland Street
Phoenix, AZ 85004
602-253-8633
Fax 602-258-6533
email:
    grandcanyon@uswest.net
http://users.uswest.net/~gehlker

Skyliner Hiking Club
1680 Rainbow Road
Cottonwood, AZ 86326
520-634-7633

Tucson Orienteering Club
PO Box 13012
Tucson, AZ 85732
http://www.bayside.net/users/cbsites/toc

ARKANSAS

Arkansas State Parks
One Capital Mall
Little Rock, AR 72201

Northeast Arkansas Striders
120 North 2nd Street
Paragould, AR 72450
870-236-6972

Ozark Highlands Trail Association
411 Patricia Lane
Fayetteville, AR 72703
501-442-2799
email:
    ohta@arkansasusa.com
http://wilderness.arkansasusa.com/ohta

Ozark Society, Inc.
PO Box 2914
Little Rock, AR 72203

CALIFORNIA

American Discovery Trail —California Section
66 Loma Vista Drive
Orinda, CA 94563
925-254-7341
Fax 925-253-0381

Amigos de Anza
1350 Castle Rock Road
Walnut Creek, CA 94598
510-937-7661
Fax 510-943-7431

Antioch Trail Masters
c/o D. Walters
PO Box 433
Antioch, CA 94509
510-778-0490
Fax 510-754-8985
email: GraysonS4@aol.com

Bay Area Ridge Trail Council
26 O'Farrell Street, Suite 400
San Francisco, CA 94108
415-391-9300
Fax 415-391-2649

California Department of Parks and Recreation
1416 9th Street, Suite 14411
Sacramento, CA 95814
916-653-7995
http://cal-parks.ca.gov

California Recreational Trails Committee
PO Box 942896
Sacramento, CA 94296
916-653-8803
Fax 916-653-4458
email: cwill@parks.ca.gov

California State Parks
PO Box 942896
Sacramento, CA 94296-0001
916-653-6995

California Trails Foundation
PO Box 183
Los Altos, CA 94023
800-325-CTGF
714-493-4222

Coastwalk
1389 Cooper Road
Sebastopol, CA 95472
800-550-6854
707-829-6689
email: coastwalk@sonic.net
http://www.sonic.net/coastwalk

**East Bay Area Trails
  Council**
PO Box 5381
Oakland, CA 94605
510-635-0138, ext. 2611
Fax 510-569-1417

**Hermosa Valley
  Greenbelt**
Community Resources
  Development
710 Pier Avenue
Hermosa Beach, CA
  90254
310-318-0280
Fax 310-372-4333

**Jamul Trails Council,
  Inc.**
PO Box 551
Jamul, CA 91935
619-669-1513
Fax 619-669-1513

JPL Trailbuilders
Caltech Y, Mail Code
  218-51
Pasadena, CA 91106
626-395-6163
Fax 626-795-9725

Lafayette Trails Group
500 St. Mary Road
Lafayette, CA 94549
510-284-2232

**Laguna Mountain
  Volunteer Association**
PO Box 250
Mt. Laguna, CA 91948
619-473-8343

**Northern San Diego
  County Regional Trails**
c/o City San Marcos
3 Civic Center Drive
San Marcos, CA 92069
760-744-9000
Fax 760-752-1328

**Rancho Simi Trail
  Blazers**
Rancho Simi Recreation
  & Park Dept.
1692 Sycamore, Drive
Simi Valley, CA 93065
805-584-4400
Fax 805-526-7648

San Francisco Bay Trail
PO Box 2050
Oakland, CA 94604
510-464-7935
Fax 510-464-7970
email: ceils@abag.ca.gov
http://www.abag.ca.gov/
  bayarea/baytrail/
  baytrail.html

**Santa Cruz Mountains
  Trail Association**
PO Box 183
Los Altos, CA 94023

**Santa Monica Mountains
  Trails Council**
PO Box 345
Agoura Hills, CA 91376
818-222-4531
Fax 818-889-4540
email:
  Ruthgerson@aol.com

**Sierra Club—San Diego
  Imperial Counties
  Chapter**
3820 Ray Street
San Diego, CA 92104
619-299-1743
Fax 619-299-1742
Bookstore phone 619-299-
  1797
email: sandiego.chapter@
  sierraclub.org
http://www.sierraclub.org/
  chapters/sandiego

Trail Center
3921 East Bayshore Road,
  Suite 205A
Palo Alto, CA 94303
650-968-7065
Fax 650-962-8234
http://www.trailcenter.org

**Western States Trail
  Foundation**
701 High Street, #228 C
Auburn, CA 95603
950-823-7282
Fax 950-823-7901
email: wstf@foothill.net
http://www.foothill.net/tevis

COLORADO

**American Discovery Trail
  —Colorado Section**
10597 N. Routt Lane
Westminster, CO 80021
303-465-1033
Fax 303-894-3398

**Colorado Division of
  Parks & Recreation**
1313 Sherman Street,
  Suite 618
Denver, CO 80203
303-866-3437
Fax 303-866-3206

Colorado Mountain Club
710 10th Street, Suite 200
Golden, CO 80401
303-279-3080

**Colorado Mountain
  Club—Boulder Group**
825 South Broadway,
  Suite 40
Boulder, CO 80303
303-554-7688

**North Fork Trails
  Network**
1146 3950 Road
Paonia, CO 81428
303-921-6400
Fax 303-921-6500

**Pikes Peak Area Trails &
  Open Space Coalition**
1426 North Hancock,
  Suite 4, North
Colorado Springs, CO
  80903
719-633-6884
Fax 719-633-7840

Summit Huts Association
PO Box 2830
Breckenridge, CO 80424
970-453-8583
Fax 970-453-8583
email: sumhuts@
  colorado.net

Uncompahgre Riverway
PO Box 34
Montrose, CO 81402
303-249-2436

**Ute Pass Corridor Trails
  Committee**
11190 Hondo Avenue,
  Box 200
Green Mountain Falls,
  CO 80819
719-684-9811
Fax 719-684-9811

**Volunteers For Outdoor
  Colorado**
600 South Marion Parkway
Denver, CO 80209
303-715-1010
Fax 303-715-1212
email: voc@voc.org
http://www.voc.org

CONNECTICUT

**Connecticut Forest and
  Park Association**
16 Meriden Road
Rockfall, CT 06481
860-346-2372
Fax 860-347-7463
email:
  conn.forest.assoc@snet.net
http://www.ctwoodlands.org

**Connecticut Greenways
  Council**
c/o Fuss and O'Neill
146 Hartford Road
Manchester, CT 06040
203-646-2469

Connecticut Trails
c/o Dick Blake
11 Argyle Road
Milford, CT 06460
203-874-8408

**DEP—State Parks
  Division, Parks and
  Recreation**
79 Elm Street
Hartford, CT 06106
860-424-3200

**Farmington Canal Rail-
  to-Trail Association**
c/o William Davies
79 Hartley Street
North Haven, CT 06473
203-281-7194
email: bdavies@snet.net

Somers Trails Association
105 Ninth District Road
Somers, CT 06071
860-749-2701
email:
　JanCollins@aol.com

**Western Connecticut
　Orienteering Club**
100 Braemar Drive
Cheshire, CT 06410
203-272-7354
email: skdewitt@aol.com
http://sunrsc.fairfield.edu/
　~rdewitt/wcoc

DELAWARE

**American Discovery Trail
　—Delaware Section**
Attn: Jim Ippolito
609 Savannah Road
Lewes, DE 19958
302-645-6378
Fax 302-645-3466
email: jacy@shore.
　intercom.net

**Delaware Department of
　Natural Resources &
　Environmental Control**
Department of Parks and
　Recreation
89 Kings Highway
Dover, DE 19901
302-739-5823
Fax 302-739-3817
http://www.dnrec.state.de.us

Wilmington Trail Club
PO Box 1184
Wilmington, DE 19899
410-287-6567

DISTRICT OF
COLUMBIA

**Department of
　Recreation and Parks**
3149 16th Street, NW,
　4th Floor
Washington, DC 20010
202-673-7665
Fax 202-673-2087

**Washington Women
　Outdoors**
7007 Ellen Avenue
Falls Church, VA 22042
Phone 301-864-3070
email: wwo@patriot.net
http://patriot.net/wwo

FLORIDA

Florida Audubon Society
1331 Palmetto Avenue,
　Suite 110
Winter Park, FL 32789
407-539-5700
Fax 407-539-5701

**Florida Department of
　Natural Resources
　Parks and Recreation**
3900 Commonwealth
　Boulevard, Sta. 585
Tallahassee, FL 32399
904-488-5372

Florida Greenways
Florida Department of
　Environmental
　Protection
3900 Commonwealth
　Bouldevard, MS-795
Tallahassee, FL 32399-
　3000
850-488-3701
Fax 850-922-6302
http://www.dep.state.fl.us

Florida Trail Association
　(call for information on
　local chapters)
PO Box 13708
Gainesville, FL 32604
800-343-1882
352-378-8823
Fax 352-378-4550
email: fta@florida-trail.org
http://www.florida-trail.
　org/~fta

**Rails-to-Trails
　Conservancy—Florida
　Field Office**
2545 Blairstone Pines
　Drive
Tallahasse, FL 32301
904-942-2379
Fax 904-942-4431

rtcoffl@aol.com
http://www.railtrails.org

**Rails-to-Trails
　Withlacoochee**
PO Box 807
Inverness, FL 34451-0807
352-726-2251

GEORGIA

**Georgia Appalachian
　Trail Club, Inc.**
PO Box 654
Atlanta, GA 30301
404-634-6495

**Georgia Department of
　Natural Resources**
Parks, Recreation and
　Historic Sites
PO Box 1029
1076 GA 356 East
Helen, GA 30545
706-878-1594
Fax 706-878-1552

**Georgia Department of
　Natural Resources**
Georgia State Parks
205 Butler Street, Suite 1352
Atlanta, GA 30334
404-656-3530
Fax 404-651-5871
http://www.gastateparks.org

HAWAII

**Hawaiian Trail and
　Mountain Club**
PO Box 2238
Honolulu, HI 96804
http://www.onesky.com/
　htmc

Kona Hiking Club
76-6298 Koholia
Kailua Kona, HI 96740
808-329-5519

IDAHO

Idaho Alpine Club
PO Box 2885
Idaho Falls, ID 83403-2885
208-524-6119
email: iac@srv.net
http://www.srv.net/~iac

**Idaho Department of
　Parks & Recreation**
PO Box 83720
Boise, ID 83720-0065
208-334-4199

Idaho Trails Council, Inc.
c/o Bernice Paige
PO Box 1629
Sun Valley, ID 83353
208-622-3046

**Sierra Club—Northern
　Rockies Chapter**
PO Box 552
Boise, ID 83701
208-384-1023
email: northern.rockies.
　chapter@sierraclub.org

ILLINOIS

**American Discovery
　Trail—Southern Illinois
　Section**
1142 Winkleman Hill
Harrisburg, IL 62946
618-439-3103

**Friends of the I and M
　Canal**
19 West 580 83rd
Downers Grove, IL 60516
630-985-3895
Fax 630-271-6566,
　attn. H. Hisgen
email: dcrazyone@aol.com

**Illinois Department of
　Natural Resources**
524 South 2nd Street,
　Suite 310
Springfield, IL 62701
217-782-7454
Fax 217-782-9599

**Openlands Project
　Greenways**
220 South State Street,
　Suite 1880
Chicago, IL 60604
312-427-4256
Fax 312-427-6251

INDIANA

American Discovery Trail—Indiana Section
4303 Greenway Drive
Indianapolis, IN 46220
317-255-6215

Cardinal Greenway
650 West Minnetrista Boulevard
Muncie, IN 47303

Friends of Pumpkinvine National Trail
PO Box 392
Goshen, IN 46526
219-533-4943
Fax 219-535-7660

Hoosier Hikers Council
PO Box 822
Indianapolis, IN 46206-0822
317-349-0204

Indiana Department of Natural Resources, Division of Outdoor Recreation
402 West Washington Street, Suite 271W
Indianapolis, IN 46204
317-232-4070
Fax 317-233-4648
email: narmstrong@dnr.state.in.us
http://www.dnr.state.in.us/outdoor/index.htm

Indianapolis Hiking Club
7129 Chandler Drive
Indianapolis, IN 46217
317-882-4760

Rails-to-Trails
PO Box 402
47 South Pennsylvania Street
Indianapolis, IN 46206
317-237-9348

Whitewater Valley Wanderers
715 College Avenue
Richmond, IN 47374

IOWA

American Discovery Trail—Iowa Section
PO Box 131
Center Point, IA 52213
319-849-1844

Cedar Valley Nature Trail
1890 County Home Road
Marion, IA 52302
319-398-3505
Fax 319-373-2213

Great Lakes Spine Trail
Dickinson County
1924 240th Street
Milford, IA 51351
712-338-4786
Fax 712-338-4786
email: dccb@rconnect.com

Great Western Trail
Polk County Conservation Board
Jester Park
Granger, IA 50109
515-999-2775
Fax 515-999-2705

Heart of Iowa Nature Trail
c/o Story County Conservation Board
56461 180th Street
Ames, IA 50010
515-232-2516
Fax 515-232-6989

Hoover Nature Trail, Inc.
PO Box 531
Muscatine, IA 52761
319-263-4043
Fax 319-263-9073

Iowa Department of Natural Resources
Parks, Recreation, & Preserves Division
Wallace State Office Building
Des Moines, IA 50319-0034
515-281-TENT

Iowa Natural Heritage Foundation
505 5th Avenue, Suite 444
Des Moines, IA 50309-2301
515-288-1846
Fax 515-288-0137
email: info@inhf.org
http://www.inhf.org

Iowa Trails Council
PO Box 131
Center Point, IA 52213
319-849-1844
Fax 319-849-2866
email: tomneenan1@aol.com

Pocahantas Conservation Board
702 NW Seventh Street
Pocahontas, IA 50574
712-335-4395
Fax 712-335-3606
email: pokyccb@ncn.net
http://www.ncn.net/~pokyccb/PCCB

Sauk Rail Trail—Carroll County Section
Carroll County Conservation Board
22811 Swan Lake Drive
Carroll, IA 51401
712-792-4614
712-792-8078

Sauk Trail—Sac County Sectionxs
Sac County Conservation Board
2970 280th Street
Sac City, IA 50583
712-662-4530
Fax 712-662-7879

Sierra Club—Iowa Chapter
3500 Kingman Boulevard
Des Moines, IA 50311
515-277-8868

Sierra Club—Northwest Iowa Chapter
30 Stewart Avenue
Sioux Falls, IA 51104
712-274-5104

Three Rivers Trail
c/o Hubolt County Conservation Board
Courthouse
Dakota City, IA 50529
515-332-4087

Winnebago County Conservation Board
34496 110th Avenue
Forest City, IA 50436
515-565-3390
515-582-2891

KANSAS

American Discovery Trail—Kansas Section
1895 East 56 Road
Lecompton, KS 66050

Haskell Rail Trail
c/o Lawrence Parks and Recreation
PO Box 708
Lawrence, KS 66044
913-832-3450
Fax 913-832-3405

Kansas Trails Council, Inc.
c/o Mark Barnes
2760 NE Sunbird Lane
Weir, KS 66781
316-396-8512

Kansas Wildlife and Parks
900 Jackson, Suite 502
Topeka, KS 66612
913-296-2281
Fax 913-296-6953

KENTUCKY

Jefferson Memorial Forest—Trail Committee
PO Box 467
11311 Mitchell Hill Road
Fairdale, KY 40118
502-368-5404
Fax 502-368-6517
email: sgoodwin@looky.org

Kentucky State Parks
Capital Plaza Tower
500 Mero Street, Suite 1100

Frankfort, KY 40601-
1974
800-255-PARK

LOUISIANA

**Louisiana Office of State
Parks**
PO Box 44426
Baton Rouge, LA 70804-
4426
800-677-1400
504-342-8111

MAINE

**Allagash Wilderness
Waterway**
PO Box 939
Millinocket, ME 04462
207-723-8518
Fax 207-723-4519
email:
timothy.caverly@state.
me.us

**Appalachian Mountain
Club—Maine Chapter**
PO Box 1534
Portland, ME 04104
617-523-0636
email:
wtemml@maine.rr.com
http://www.gwi.net/
amcmaine
http://www.outdoors.org

**Bureau of Parks and
Lands**
Conservation Department
State House, Station 22
Augusta, ME 04333
207-287-3821
Fax 207-287-6170
campground reservations:
800-332-1501
http://www.state.me.us/
doc.home.htm

**College Conservation
Corps of Maine**
124 HSH
Augusta, ME 04333
207-287-6107
Fax 207-287-3611
email: corps.conservation@
state.me.us

http://www.agate.net/
~editec

**Kennebec Valley Tourism
Council**
179 Main Street
Waterville, ME 04901
800-393-8629
http://www.mint.net/
mainevacation

Maine Audubon Society
PO Box 6009
Falmouth, ME 04105
207-781-2330
Fax 207-781-6155

**Maine Island Trail
Association**
PO Box C
Rockland, ME 04841
207-596-6456
islands@ime.net
http://www.mita.org

**Maine Trails Advisory
Committee**
c/o Maine Bureau of Parks
& Lands
22 State House Station
Augusta, ME 04333
207-287-2163
Fax 207-287-3823

Moriah Brook Trail
RR 2 Box 2270
Bethel, ME 04217

Portland Trails
1 India Street
Portland, ME 04101
207-775-2411
Fax 207-772-7673
email: info@trails.org
http://www.trails.org

**Sierra Club—Maine
Chapter**
192 State Street
Portland, ME 04101-3712
207-761-5616

MARYLAND

**American Discovery
Trail—Maryland/DC**
3008 Tarragon Lane
Bowie, MD 20715

**Baltimore & Annapolis
Trail Park**
PO Box 1007
Severna Park, MD 21146
410-222-6244

**Chesapeake and Ohio
Canal Association**
PO Box 366
Glen Echo, MD 20812
301-983-0825

**Friendly Trails
Wandering Club**
5457 Enberend Terrace
Columbia, MD 21045
410-715-0912
Fax 410-992-4665
email: BauerTravel@
compuserve.com

**Maryland Department of
Natural Resources**
580 Taylor Avenue
Tawes State Office
Building
Annapolis, MD 21401
800-830-3974

**Seneca Valley Sugar
Loafers**
1830 Greenplace Road
Rockville, MD 20850
301-340-9418
Fax 301-530-8659
email: desta2@aol.com

MASSACHUSETTS

**Andover Trails
Committee**
c/o Bay Circuit Alliance
3 Railroad Street
Andover, MA 01810
978-470-1982
email:
baycircuit@juno.com
http://www.serve.com/
baycircuit

**Appalachian Mountain
Club—Berkshire
Chapter**
PO Box 9369
North Amherst, MA
01059-9369
413-596-9643

Fax 413-549-3621
http://www.unix.oit.umass.
edu/~berkame

**Appalachian Mountain
Club—Boston Chapter**
47 Prospect Street
Newburyport, MA 01950
508-465-1844
Fax 508-465-1844

Bay Circuit Alliance
Alan French, Chair
3 Railroad Street
Andover, MA 01810
508-470-1982

**Berkshire Natural
Resources Council**
20 Bank Row
Pittsfield, MA 01201
413-499-0596
Fax 413-499-3924
email: bnrc@bcn.net

Broad Brook Coalition
PO Box 60566
Florence, MA 01060
http://www.shore.net/
~mltc

**Cape Cod Trails
Conference**
81 Maple Lane
Brewster, MA 02631-2115
508-255-3717
email: cctrails@cape.com
http://www.vst.cape.com/
~cctrails

Chiltern Mountain Club
PO Box 407
Boston, MA 02117-0407
888-831-3100
617-859-2843

**Essex County Trails
Association**
PO Box 947
Essex, MA 01929
978-356-7656

Friends of Blue Hills
1894 Canton Avenue
Milton, MA 02186
617-326-0079

Friends of the Warner Trail
30 Water Street
Oxborough, MA 02035
508-543-2633

Massachusetts Audubon Society
Lincoln, MA 01773
781-259-9500
800-AUDUBON
Fax 781-259-8899
http://www.massaudubon.org

Massachusetts State Forests & Parks
100 Cambridge Street
Boston, MA 02202
617-727-3180
Fax 617-727-9402

Metacomet Monadnock Trail
c/o Patrick Fletcher
20 Linda Drive
Westfield, MA 01085
413-562-9863

MICHIGAN

North Country Trail Association
49 Monroe Center, Suite 200B
Grand Rapids, MI 49503
616-454-5506
Fax 616-454-7139

Sierra Club—Mackinac Chapter
300 North Washington Square, Suite 411
Lansing, MI 48933-1223
517-484-2372
Fax 517-484-3108
email: mackinac.
  chapter@sierraclub.org

Rails-to-Trails Conservancy— Michigan Chapter
913 West Holmes, Suite 145
Lansing, MI 48910
517-393-6022
Fax 517-393-1960
email: rtcmich@aol.com
http://www.railtrail.org

MINNESOTA

Kekekabic Trail Club
309 Cedar Avenue South
Minneapolis, MN 55454
800-818-HIKE

Minnesota Department of Natural Resources, Parks & Recreation Division
500 Lafayette Road
St. Paul, MN 55155-4040
612-296-9223

Minnesota Orienteering Club
PO Box 580030
Minneapolis, MN 55458
507-334-8140

Minnesota Parks and Trails Council
PO Box 26243
St. Paul, MN 55126
612-631-2818
Fax 612-631-2617

Minnesota Women's Directory
771 Raymond Avenue
St. Paul, MN 55114
612-646-3968
Fax 612-646-2186
email: directory@
  womenspress.com
http://www.womenspress.
  com/dir/dir.html

Superior Hiking Trail Association
PO Box 4
731 Seventh Avenue
Two Harbors, MN 55616
218-834-2700
Fax 218-834-4436
email: swphike@mr.net
http://www.shta.org

MISSOURI

American Discovery Trail—Missouri Section
1001 East Walnut Street, Suite 300
Columbia, MO 65201
314-449-5227
Fax 314-449-7678

Missouri Department of Natural Resources, Division of State Parks
PO Box 176
Jefferson City, MO 65102
800-334-6946
573-751-2479
Fax 573-751-8656
email: moparks@mail.state.
  mo.us
http://www.state.mo.us/
  dnr/dsp/homedsp.htm

Ozark Greenways, Inc.
PO Box 50733
Springfield, MO 65805
417-864-2015
Fax 417-864-1497
email: ozarkgreenways@
  ci.springfield.mo.us

Gateway Trailnet
3900 Reavis Barracks Road
St. Louis, MO 63125
314-416-9930
Fax 314-416-9928

MONTANA

Greater Yellowstone Coalition
PO Box 1874
Bozeman, MT 59771
800-775-1834
406-586-1593
Fax 406-586-0851
email: gyc@gyc.desktop.org
http://www.desktop.org/gyc

Montana Fish, Wildlife, and Parks
PO Box 200701
1420 East Sixth Avenue
Helena, MT 59620
406-444-2585
email: fwpgen@mt.gov

Rivers Edge Trail
PO Box 553
Great Falls, MT 59403
406-761-4966
email: trailsrus@
  in-tch.com

Sierra Club—Montana Chapter
c/o Sherm Janke
415 North 17th Avenue
Bozeman, MT 59715-3109
406-587-9782

NEBRASKA

American Discovery Trail—Nebraska Section
3340 South 29th Street
Lincoln, NE 68502
402-421-1401
Fax 402-421-1463

Iron Horse Trail Lake Park
Nemaha NRD
125 Jackson
Tecumseh, NE 68450
402-335-3325
Fax 402-335-3265

Nebraska Game and Parks Commission
2200 North 33rd Street
Lincoln, NE 68503
402-471-0641

Sierra Club—Nebraska Chapter
c/o Mary Anna Anderson
7020 Burt Street
Omaha, NE 68132-2611
402-551-7223
email:
  CocoFlower@aol.com

NEVADA

American Discovery Trail—Nevada Section
649 East Appion Way
Carson City, NV 89701
702-885-7825

Nevada Division of State Parks
1300 South Curry Street
Carson City, NV 89701
702-687-4370
Fax 702-687-4117

Sierra Club—Toiyabe Chapter
PO Box 8096
Reno, NV 89507
702-747-7141

Tahoe Rim Trail Fund, Inc.
PO Box 4647
Stateline, NV 89449
702-588-0686
Fax 702-588-8737
email: TahoeRim@aol.com
http://www.yaws.com/LakeTahoe/trt.shtml

NEW HAMPSHIRE

AMC—New Hampshire Chapter
c/o D. Kurt Piper
70 Burnt Hill Road
Weare, NH 03281
603-529-4390 (7–9 P.M.)

Androscoggin/Evans Notch Ranger District
300 Glen Road
Gorham, NH 03581

Cardigan Highlanders
PO Box 104
Enfield Center, NH 03749
603-632-5640

Chatham Trails Association
PO Box 605
Center Conway, NH 03813
978-256-9184
Fax 978-371-2287

Friends of The Wapack, Inc.
PO Box 115
West Peterborough, NH 03468
603-878-1000
email: christensen@catlas.mv.com
To be trailwork volunteer:
rick@blanchette.mv.com

Monadnock-Sunapee Greenway Trail Club
PO Box 164
Marlow, NH 03456

603-357-2115 (Tim Symonds)
Fax 603-446-7543

New Hampshire Division of Parks and Recreation
PO Box 1856
172 Pembroke Road
Concord, NH 03302
603-271-3556

NEW JERSEY

Adirondack Mountain Club—New York/New Jersey Chapter
c/o Mary Beth Becker
5 Tudor City Place
New York, NY 10017
212-986-1430

ADK Keene Valley Chapter
333 Dutchtown Road
Skillman, NJ 08558
908-559-2680
Fax 908-821-6655
email:
PHirschNJ@aol.com
http://www.adk.org

Adventures For Women
PO Box 515
Montvale, NJ 07645
201-930-0557
email:
AfW@FitnessOutdoors.com
http://www.FitnessOutdoors.com

Appalachian Mountain Club—New Jersey Chapter
c/o J. Arbuckle
40 Kingwood Drive
Little Falls, NJ 07424

Hunterdon Hiking Club
Hunterdon County Park
1020 Route 31
Lebanon, NJ 08833
908-806-7147

Morris Parks and Land Conservancy
44 Market Street
Morristown, NJ 07960
201-292-2572

New York/New Jersey Trails Conference
232 Madison Avenue, Suite 401
New York, NY 10016
212-685-9699
Fax 212-779-8102

Ocean County Hiking Club
Wells Mills County Park
905 Wells Mill Road, Rt. 532
Waretown, NJ 08758
609-971-3085
Fax 609-971-9540

Outdoor Club of South Jersey
PO Box 455
Cherry Hill, NJ 08003-0455
609-427-7777

Sierra Club—Loantaka Chapter
c/o Steve Ember
228 Cold Spring Court
Somerset, NJ 08873

Sierra Club—New Jersey Chapter
57 Mountain Street
Princeton, NJ 08540-2611
609-924-3141

Sierra Club—North Jersey Group
c/o Linda Issac
47 Fellswood Drive
Livingston, NJ 07039

Sierra Club—West Jersey Chapter
9 Randolph Drive
Mount Holly, NJ 08060-1142
609-267-7052

Trails For New Jersey
101 Overbrook Road
Piscataway, NJ 08854

Union County Hiking Club
69 Ethan Drive
Murray Hill, NJ 07974
908-464-8289

NEW MEXICO

New Mexico State Parks and Recreation
PO Box 1147
2040 South Pacheco
Santa Fe, NM 87504
888-NM-PARKS
505-827-7173
Fax 505-827-1376
http://www.emnrd.state.nm.us/nmparks

New Mexico Volunteers for the Outdoors
PO Box 36246
Albuquerque, NM 87176
505-884-1991

Sierra Club—Rio Grande Chapter
c/o John Buchser
606 Alto
Santa Fe, NM 87501

NEW YORK

Adirondack Mountain Club (ADK)
814 Goggins Road
Lake George, NY 12845
518-668-4447
800-395-8080
orders only)
Fax 518-668-3746
email: adkinfo@adk.org
http://www.adk.org

Adirondack Mountain Club—New York/New Jersey Chapter
c/o Mary Beth Becker
5 Tudor City Place
New York, NY 10017
212-986-1430

Adirondack Forty-Sixers, Inc.
279 Rand Hill Road
Morrisonville, NY 12962-9732
518-563-2973

The Catskill Center for Conservation and Development, Inc.
Route 28
Arkville, NY 12406

914-586-2611
Fax 914-586-3044
email: cccd@catskill.net
http://www.catskillcenter.org

**Central New York
Orienteering**
6187 Smith Road
North Syracuse, NY
13212
315-458-6406
email: bsleight@aol.com
http://cnyo.us.orienteering.
org/cnyo

**Cresent Trail Hiking
Association**
PO Box 1354
Fairport, NY 14450
716-234-1620
http://www.ggw.org/freenet/
c/ctha

**Dutchess-Putnam
County—Appalachian
Trail Management
Committee**
(Part of New York/New
Jersey Trail Conference)
232 Madison Avenue,
Room 802
New York, NY 10016
212-685-9699
Fax 212-779-8102
email: nynjtc@aol.com
http://www.nynjtc.org

**Finger Lakes Trail
Conference FLTA)**
PO Box 18048
Rochester, NY 14618-0048
716-288-7191
Fax 716-288-7191 call
ahead)
email: fltr@axsnet.com
http://www.fingerlakes.net/
trailsystem

**Genesee Valley Hiking
Club**
16 Merwin Avenue
Rochester, NY 14609
716-224-9775

**German American
Hiking Club**
c/o E. Hoyer

42-51 Ketcham Street
Elmhurst, NY 11373
718-457-8319
email: ehoyer@usa.net

**Hudson Valley
Orienteering**
PO Box 61
Pleasantville, NY 10570
973-625-0499
email: hvo@juno.com
http://www.geocities.com/
Yosemite/8761

**Long Island Greenbelt
Trail Conference**
c/o Michelle Black
23 Deer Path Road
Central Islip, NY 11722
516-360-0753
Trail information center:
516-369-9768
Fax 516-360-0753

Mohonk Preserve
PO Box 715
New Paltz, NY 12561
914-255-0919
Fax 914-255-5646
http://mohonkpreserve.
mhv.net

**New York/New Jersey
Trail Conference**
232 Madison Avenue,
Room 802
New York, NY 10016
212-685-9699
Fax 212-779-8102
email: nynjtc@aol.com
http://www.nynjtc.org

New York State Parks
Albany, NY 12238
518-474-0456

New York State Trails
c/o Minnewaska State
Park Preserve
PO Box 893
New Paltz, NY 12561
email: minne@netstep.net

Rip Van Winkle Hikers
65 Main Street
Saugerties, NY 12477
email: RVWHikers@aol.com

Shorewalkers Inc.
Box 20748
Cathedral Station
New York, NY 10025
212-330-7686

**Sierra Club—Atlantic
Chapter**
353 Hamilton Street
Albany, NY 12210
518-426-9144

**Sierra Club—Long Island
Chapter**
PO Box 210
Syosset, NY 11791-0210
516-841-2142
email:
wily@compuserve.com

**The Skinnydippers
Nudist Club**
51-04 39th Avenue
Woodside, NY 11377-
3145
718-651-4689
Fax 718-424-1883

The Taconic Hiking Club
c/o Katharine Wolfe
45 Kakely Street
Albany, NY 12208
518-482-0424

NORTH CAROLINA

**Balsam Highland Task
Force**
103 Surrey Road NE
Mountains To Sea
Waynesville, NC 27675
704-456-3392
email: dhammett@
primeline.com

Carolina Mountain Club
PO Box 68
Asheville, NC 28802
704-693-8258

**North Carolina Bartram
Trail Society**
PO Box 144
Scaly Mountain, NC 28775
704-526-4904

**North Carolina Division
of Parks and Recreation**
PO Box 27687
Raleigh, NC 27611-7687
919-846-9991
Fax 919-870-6843
http://ils.unc.edu/
parkproject/ncparks.html

**North Carolina Rails-to-
Trails**
PO Box 61348
Durham, NC 27715-1348

**Triangle Greenways
Council**
PO Box 2746
Raleigh, NC 27602
919-828-5242
http://www.geo.duke.edu/
tgc.htm

NORTH DAKOTA

**North Dakota Parks &
Recreation Department**
1835 East Bismarck
Expressway
Bismarck, ND 58504
701-328-5357
Fax 701-328-5363

**Sierra Club—Dacotah
Chapter**
c/o Todd Herreid
RR 4 Box 82
Williston, ND 58801-9222
701-774-8904

OHIO

**American Discovery
Trail—Ohio/Kentucky
Section**
7 Peabody Drive
Oxford, OH 45056
513-523-4851

**Buckeye Trail
Association**
PO Box 254
Worthington, OH 43085
419-447-5464

Cleveland Hiking Club
PO Box 347097
Cleveland, OH 44134-7097
216-884-0281

**Columbus Outdoor
  Pursuits**
PO Box 14384
Columbus, OH 43214
614-447-1006

Metro Dayton Hikers
c/o E.W. DeLaet
138 Bonita Drive
Dayton, OH 45415
937-275-8972

**Metro Parks, Serving
  Summit County**
975 Treaty Line Road
Akron, OH 44313
330-867-5511
Fax 330-867-4711

**North Coast Inland Trail
  Conservancy**
c/o Steve Gruner
Sandusky County Parks
1950 Countryside Place
Fremont, OH 43420
419-334-4495

**Northeast Ohio
  Council—American
  Youth Hostel**
Stanford House
6093 Stanford Road
Peninsula, OH 44264-9613
330-467-8711

**Northwestern Ohio
  Rails-to-Trails**
PO Box 234
Delta, OH 43515
800-951-4788
419-822-4788

**Ohio Department of
  Natural Resources**
Fountain Square Bldg. C 4
Columbus, OH 43224
614-265-6402
Fax 614-267-4764

Orienteering Cincinnati
5412 College Corner Road
  #113
Oxford, OH 45056-1031
513-523-9279

Rails-to-Trails of Ohio
65 East Wilson Bridge
  Road, #203

Worthington, OH 43085
614-841-1075
Fax 614-841-9857

**Sierra Club—Ohio
  Chapter**
145 North High Street,
  Suite 409
Columbus, OH 43215
614-461-0734
Fax 614-461-0730

Transplant Trotters
4245 East Galbraith Road
Cincinnati, OH 45236
513-793-7755

**U.C. Mountaineering
  Club**
217 TUC
University of Cincinnati
Cincinnati, OH 45221

OKLAHOMA

**Oklahoma Department of
  Tourism and Recreation**
15 North Robinson,
  Suite 801
Oklahoma City, OK 73102
800-652-6552
405-521-2409
Fax 405-521-3992
  or 405-236-0205
email: information@
  travelok.com
http://www.travelok.com

**Sierra Club—Oklahoma
  Chapter**
PO Box 60644
Oklahoma City, OK
  73146-0644

OREGON

**Oregon Parks and
  Recreation, Trails
  Coordinator**
1115 Commercial Street
  NE
Salem, OR 97310
503-378-6378, ext. 246
Fax 503-378-6447
email:
  peter.d.bond@state.or.us

PENNSYLVANIA

Allegheny Outdoor Club
c/o John Shinaberger
1279 High Street
Bradford, PA 16701
814-368-6728

**Allegheny Valley Land
  Trust**
PO Box 777
222 Market Street
Kittanning, PA 16201
724-543-4478
Fax 724-545-9012
email: armtrail@alltel.net

**Allegheny Valley Trails
  Association**
153 South Sixth Avenue
Clarion, PA 16214
814-226-2576

Allentown Hiking Club
PO Box 1542
Allentown, PA 18105-1542
610-250-7779

**Appalachian Mountain
  Club—Delaware Valley
  Chapter**
1180 Greenleaf Drive
Bethlehem, PA 18017
610-694-8677

Arrowhead Trail
610 East McMurray Road
McMurray, PA 15317

Batona Hiking Club
c/o Bette Irwin
150 North Bethlehem
  Pike D 10
Ambler, PA 19002
215-646-3548

**Berks County
  Conservancy**
960 Old Mill Road
Wyomissing, PA 19610
610-372-4992
email: berkscon@ptd.net
http://www.
  berks-conservancy.org

**Blue Mountain Eagle
  Hiking and Climbing
  Club**
PO Box 14982
Reading, PA 19612
215-678-5564

Conewago Trail
Lancaster County Parks
  and Recreation
1050 Rockford Road
Lancaster, PA 17602
717-299-8215
Fax 717-295-5942
http://
  www.co.Lancaster.pa.us

**Delaware Valley
  Orienteering
  Association**
14 Lake Drive
Spring City, PA 19475-
  2721
610-792-0502
email: frankdvoa@aol.com
http://www.dvoa.us.
  orienteering.org

**Indiana University of
  Pennsylvania
  Orienteering Club**
c/o LTC Timothy Gilbert
110 Concord Street
Indiana, PA 15701-2405
724-349-1408
email:
  jlwolfe@grove.iup.edu
http://www.iup.edu/
  ~jlwolfe/iupoc.htm

**Keystone Trails
  Association**
PO Box 251
Cogan Station, PA 17728

Lancaster Hiking Club
c/o Jeff Brethauer
PO Box 7922
Lancaster, PA 17604
717-684-4474
email: jeff@fandm.edu

**Mason Dixon Trail
  System**
Bank Hill Road
Wrightsville, PA 17368

**Mid State Trail
Association**
PO Box 167
Boalsburg, PA 16827
814-237-7703
email: tthwaites@aol.com
or shorthiker@aol.com

Mill Creek Loop Trail
Ridgway Road
RD 1 Box 28A
Ridgway, PA 15853

Montour Trail Council
PO Box 11866
Pittsburgh, PA 15228
412-831-2030
http://trfn.clpgh.org./mtc

**Northeast Backpacking
& Hiking Club**
c/o Charles E. Horn III
218 Persimmon Lane
Elizabethtown, PA 17022
717-361-8763

**Octorara Area Trail
Society**
560 Bethel Road
Oxford, PA 19363
717-529-2786

**Pennsylvania Bureau of
State Parks**
Dept. of Conservation &
Natural Resources
PO Box 8551
Harrisburg, PA 17105-8551
888-PA-PARKS
717-772-0239
Fax 717-787-8817
email:
enved.sp@a1.dcnr.state.
pa.us
http://www.dcnr.state.pa.us

**Pennsylvania Field
Office, Rails-to-Trails
Conservancy**
105 Locust Street
Harrisburg, PA 17101
717-238-1717
Fax 717-238-7566
email: rtcofpa@aol.com

Philadelphia Trail Club
c/o Gerald Rushler
511 Sharpless Road
Springfield, PA 19064

**Rail Trail Council of
Northeast Pennsylvania**
PO Box 123
Forest City, PA 18421
717-785-7245
Fax 717-785-7244
email: tccrail@epix.net

Roaring Run Trail
c/o Watershed Association
PO Box 40
Spring Church, PA 15686

**Schuylkill Conservation
District**
7197 Fairlane Village Mall
Pottsville, PA 17901
717-429-1529
Fax 717-429-0698

**Schuylkill River
Greenway Association**
960 Old Mill Road
Wyomissing, PA 19610
610-372-3916
Fax 610-372-8624
email: srga@ptd.net

**Sierra Club—Allegheny
Group**
210 College Park Drive
Monroeville, PA 15146
724-327-8737
email:
bsundquist1@juno.com
http://www.envirolink.org/
orgs/allegheny-sc

**Sierra Club—
Pennsylvania Chapter**
600 North Second Street,
Box 663
Harrisburg, PA 17108-
0663
717-232-0101

**Susquehanna
Appalachian Trail Club,
Inc.**
PO Box 61001
Harrisburg, PA 17106-1001
717-564-1447

**Susquehanna Trailers
Hiking Club**
c/o Ed Zukauskas
108 Washington Street
Exeter, PA 18643
717-693-3773

**Wissahickon Restoration
Volunteers**
5730 Rising Sun Avenue
Philadelphia, PA 19120
215-342-8394

York Hiking Club
c/o Pat O'Dell
2684 Forest Road
York, PA 17402
717-244-6769

RHODE ISLAND

**East Coast Greenways
Alliance**
481 Post Road
Wakefield, RI 02879
401-789-1706
Fax 401-789-1706
email:
kvotava935@aol.com
http://www.greenway.org

**North South Trail
Council**
c/o Department of
Environmental
Management
Planning Division
235 Promenade Street
Providence, RI 02908
401-222-2776
Fax 401-222-2069

**Rhode Island Department
of Environmental
Management, Division
of Planning &
Development**
235 Promenade Street
Providence, RI 02908
401-222-2776
Fax 401-222-2069

**Sierra Club—Rhode
Island Chapter**
10 Abbott Park Place,
4th Floor

Providence, RI 02903-
3700
401-521-4734
Fax 401-331-5266

SOUTH CAROLINA

**Foothills Trail
Conference**
PO Box 3041
Greenville, SC 29602
864-467-9537
Fax 864-297-9568

**Sierra Club—South
Carolina Chapter**
PO Box 2388
1314 Lincoln Street
Columbia, SC 29202
800-944-8733
803-256-8487
Fax 803-256-8448
email:
scsierra@conterra.com
http://www.microbyte.net/
sierra/scscindex.htm

**South Carolina Parks,
Recreation, and
Tourism**
Division of Recreation
1205 Pendleton Street
Columbia, SC 29201
803-734-0122
Fax 803-734-1042

**South Carolina State
Trails Program**
1205 Pendleton Street
Columbia, SC 29201
http://www.sctrails.net

SOUTH DAKOTA

**South Dakota State
Parks**
523 East Capitol Avenue
Pierre, SD 57501
605-773-3391
Fax 605-773-6245
http://www.state.sd.us/gfp/

**Sierra Club—South
Dakota Chapter**
PO Box 1624
Rapid City, SD 57709-1624
605-348-1345
Fax 605-348-1344

TENNESSEE

Chattanooga Hiking Club
PO Box 1443
Chattanooga, TN 37403

Sierra Club—Tennessee Chapter
c/o Shiela Shay
2408 Belmont Boulevard, Apt. A3
Nashville, TN 37212-5504
615-298-5154

Tennessee Eastman Hiking and Camping Club
c/o Eastman Employee Center
PO Box 511
Kingsport, TN 37662
615-229-1484
Fax 615-229-4558
http://kpt1.tricon.net/Org/tehcc

Tennessee Trails Association
PO Box 41446
Nashville, TN 37204
615-852-4777
http://www.tn-trails.org

TEXAS

Houston Orienteering Club
PO Box 18251
Houston, TX 77023
713-484-1391
email:
    cortegon@phoenix.net
http://c-com.net/
    ~cortegon

Lone Star Trail Hiking Club
PO Box 3021
Houston, TX 77253-3021

Save Barton Creek Association
PO Box 5923
Austin, TX 78763
512-328-2481
Fax 512-367-2533
email:
    geocofer@swbell.net

http://www.austin360.com/comm/sbca/index.htm

Sierra Club—Lone Star Chapter
PO Box 1931
Austin, TX 78767
512-477-1729

Texas Parks & Wildlife Department
4200 Smith School Road
Austin, TX 78744
512-389-4735
Fax 512-389-4469
http://www.tpwd.state.tx.us

UTAH

American Discovery Trail—Utah Section
PO Box 1590
Beaver, UT 84713
435-438-5959
Fax 435-438-2112
email: xcalfire@aol.com

Castle County Canyoneers
PO Box 255
Price, Utah 84501

Cedar City Trails Council
PO Box 249
286 North Main
Cedar City, UT 84720
435-865-9223

Mountain Trails Foundation
PO Box 754
Park City, UT 84060
435-649-6839

North View Trails Committee
2850 North 1000 West
Ogden, UT 84414
801-782-3947
Fax 801-737-9734
email: gbarkerpv@aol
    .com

Sierra Club—Utah Chapter
2273 South Highland Drive, Suite 2D

Salt Lake City, UT 84106-2832
801-467-9267
email: utah.chapter@
    sierraclub.org

Utah Division of Parks and Recreation
PO Box 146001
1594 West North Temple, Suite 116
Salt Lake City, UT 84116
801-538-7220
Fax 801-538-7378
http://www.nr.state.ut.us/parks/utahstpk.htm

Utah Historic Trails Consortium
300 Rio Grande
Salt Lake City, UT 84101

Utah State Parks & Recreation
1594 West North Temple, Suite 116
Salt Lake City, UT 84114-6001
801-538-7220

Utah Trails Council
Weber County Planning/Municipal Suite 714
Ogden, UT 84401

VERMONT

Green Mountain Club, Inc.
c/o Dennis Shafer
Route100
Waterbury Center, VT 05677
802-244-7037

National Audubon Society—Vermont State Office
65 Millet Street
Richmond, VT 05477
802-434-4300

Sierra Club—Vermont Chapter
PO Box 5668
Essex Junction, VT 05453-5568
802-658-5782

email: vermont.chapter@
    sierraclub.org

Vermont Department of Forests, Parks, & Recreation
103 South Main Street
Waterbury, VT 05671-0601
802-241-3670
Fax 802-244-1481

VIRGINIA

Capital Hiking Club
3324 Glenmore Drive
Falls Church, VA 22041
703-578-1942
email: caphiker@aol.com
http://www.teleport.com/
    ~walking/chc.shtml

Center Hiking Club
c/o Michael McClain
5367 Holmes Run Parkway
Alexandria, VA 22304

Natural Bridge Appalachian Trail Club
PO Box 3012
Lynchburg, VA 24503
804-237-4015
email: Happifeet@aol.com
http://www.inmind.com/nbatc

Old Dominion Appalachian Trail Club
PO Box 25283
Richmond, VA 23260

Potomac Appalachian Trail Club
118 Park Street, SE
Vienna, VA 22180
703-242-0693
Fax 703-240-0968
http://patc.simplenet.com/

Potomac Backpacker Association
PO Box 403
Merrifield, VA 22116-0403
703-524-1185

Quantico Orienteering Club
6212 Thomas Drive
Springfield, VA 22150-1220
703-528-INFO
email:
sidneysachs@juno.com
http://axsamer.org/~sachs/
qoc.htm

Sierra Club—Virginia Chapter
PO Box 14648
Richmond, VA 23221-0648
804-722-5550

Tidewater Appalachian Trail Club
PO Box 8246
Norfolk, VA 23503
804-423-2832, ext. 278
Fax 804-489-3716

Virginia Department of Conservation and Recreation
203 Governor Street, Suite 326
Richmond, VA 23219
804-786-5492
Fax 804-786-6141
email: wjc@ocr.state.va.us
http://www.state.va.us/~dcr

Virginia Trail Conservatory
792 Boliver Road
Fort Valley, VA 22652
540-933-6071

WASHINGTON

Alpine Lakes Protection Society
c/o Forrest W. Walls
701 5th Avenue, Suite 5000
Seattle, WA 98104
206-783-6666 (Len Gardner)
email: len.gardner@
ci.seattle.wa.us
http://members.aol.com/
alpinelps/index.html

Cascade Orienteering Club
PO Box 31375
Seattle, WA 98103

206-783-3866
http://www.eskimo
.com/shelter.com/
orienteering/pnw.html

Foothills Rails-to-Trails Coalition
617 5th Avenue, NW
Puyallup, WA 98371
206-841-2570
email: Bugtrail@aol.com
http://pages.prodigy.com/
WA/foothills

Issaquah Alps Trails Club
PO Box 351
Issaquah, WA 98027

Kettle Range Conservation Group
PO Box 150
Republic, WA 99166
509-775-2667
http://www.televar.com/
~tcoleman

Lake Roosevelt National Recreation Area
1008 Crest Drive
Coulee Dam, WA 99116
509-633-9441
Fax 509-633-9332

Methow Valley Sport Trails Association
PO Box 147
Winthrop, WA 98862
206-996-3287
Fax 509-996-3282
Trail info: 800-682-5787
email:
mvsta@methow.com
http://www.methow.com/
~mvsta/

Mountains To Sound Greenway
506 Second Avenue, Suite 1502
Seattle, WA 98104
206-382-5565
Fax 206-382-3414
email:
MTSGreenway@tpl.org
http://www.front-
street.com/comorg/
mountains/2sound.htm

Pacific Northwest Trail Association
1361 Avon Allen Road
Mount Vernon, WA 98273

Redmond Trails Committee
15965 NE 85th Street
Redmond, WA 98052
206-556-2327
Fax 206-556-2303

State of Washington Interagency Committee for Outdoor Recreation
PO Box 40917
Olympia, WA 98504
206-902-3000
Fax 206-902-3026

Washington State Parks & Recreation Commission
PO Box 42650
Olympia, WA 98504
800-233-0321

Washington Trails Association
1305 Fourth Avenue, Suite 512
Seattle, WA 98101-2401
206-625-1367
Fax 206-625-9249
email: wta@halcyon.com
http://www.wta.org/wta

Washington Water Trails Association
4649 Sunnyside Avenue North, Suite 305
Seattle, WA 98103-6900
206-545-9161
email:
wwta@eskimo.com
http://www.eskimo.com/
~wwta

Yakima Greenway Foundation
111 South 18th Street
Yakima, WA 98901
509-453-8290
Fax 509-453-0318
email:
greenway@nwinfo.net

Yakima Valley Audubon Society
PO Box 2823
Yakima, WA 98907
509-457-8122
email: birdin@aol.com

WEST VIRGINIA

American Discovery Trails—West Virginia Section
1202 Ridge Drive
South Charleston, WV 25309
304-768-0528

Elk River Trail
Kanawha Parks and Recreation
2000 Coonskin Drive
Charleston, WV 25311
304-341-8000
Fax 304-344-2696

Mary Ingles Trail Blazers
PO Box 780
Poca, WV 25139
304-696-7315

North Bend Rails-to-Trails Foundation
PO Box 206
Cairo, WV 26337
800-899-6278
304-643-2500

West Virginia Development Office
Capital Complex, Building 6, Room 553
Charleston, WV 25305
800-982-3386
304-558-4010
Fax 304-558-3248
email: wvdo@wvdo.org
http://www.wvdo.org

West Virginia Scenic Trails Association
PO Box 4042
Charleston, WV 25364
304-466-2724

Wheeling Bicycle-Jogging Path
305 City Building
1500 Chapline Street

Wheeling, WV 26003
304-234-3701
Fax 304-234-3899
email: dod@hgo.net

**West Virginia Trails
Coalition**
PO Box 487
Nitro, WV 25143
304-755-4878

WISCONSIN

Chippewa River Trail
1300 First Avenue
Eau Claire, WI 54703
715-839-5032
Fax 715-839-1685

Elroy Sparta Trail
PO Box 99
Ontario, WI 54651
608-337-4775

The "400" State Trail
c/o Wildcat Mountain
   State Park
PO Box 99
Ontario, WI 54651
608-337-4775

**Sierra Club—Fox Valley
Group**
815 East Washington
Appleton, WI 54302
414-739-6041
email: fvsg@focol.org

**Friends of Glacial
Drumlin Trail**
c/o Lake Mills Depot
1213 South Main
Lake Mills, WI 53551
920-648-8774
Fax 920-648-5166
email:
   whited@dnr.state.wi.us

**Ice Age Park and Trail
Foundation**
PO Box 423
Pewaukee, WI 53072
800-227-0046
414-691-2776
Fax 414-691-2323
email: iat@execpc.com
http://www.iceagetrail.org

**Madeline Island
Wilderness Preserve**
PO Box 28
La Pointe, WI 54850-0028

**Sierra Club—John Muir
Chapter**
222 South Hamilton
   Street, #1
Madison, WI 53703-3201
608-256-0565

**Tri-County Recreational
Corridor**
PO Box 1174
Superior, WI 54880

715-395-0358
Fax 218-724-2165

**Wisconsin Bureau of
Parks and Recreation**
PO Box 7921
Madison, WI 53707
608-266-2181
Fax 608-267-7474
email:
   wiparks@dnr.state.wi.us
http://www.dnr.state.wi.us/
   org/land/parks

Wisconsin Go Hiking Club
414-299-9285

Wisconsin Hoofers
800 Langdon Street
Madison, WI 53706
608-265-4663
Fax 608-262-5467

WYOMING

The Bear Project, Inc.
1200 Main Street
Evanston, WY 82930
800-328-9708
307-789-9805
Fax 307-789-4109
email:planning@allwest.net

Clear Creek Pathway
701 Circle Drive
Buffalo, WY 82834
307-684-2991

**Greater Cheyenne
Greenway**
2101 O'Neil Avenue
Cheyenne, WY 82001
307-637-6285
Fax 307-637-6454

**Sierra Club—Wyoming
Chapter**
c/o Scott Thomas
1145 Mountain View
   Avenue
Rawlins, WY 82301
307-324-7191

**Wyoming Division of
State Parks and
Historic Sites**
122 West 25th Street
Herschler Building, 1-E
Cheyenne, WY 82002
307-777-6323
Fax 307-777-6472
email:
   sphs@missc.state.wy.us
http://commerce.state.
   wy.us/sphs/index1.htm

AN EQUIPMENT CHECKLIST

Every time I pack for a trip, I review the following equipment checklist to make sure I haven't left anything out. Don't plan on taking every item on this list on every trip. Instead, go through each category and select the gear that is necessary for the kind of trip you plan to take. You may need more of one item, such as warm clothes for a cold-weather trip, and you may leave out some items altogether, such as bug repellent on a winter camping trip.

Basic gear

backpack with rain fly
tent with rain fly and ground cloth
sleeping bag
mattress pad
water bottle

water bag
mini-flashlight or headlamp
small pocket knife
maps and guides

first aid kit (contents listed below)
money
identification

Clothing

boots
hiking socks
gaiters
camp shoes (sandals or
   sneakers)

underwear/bra
long underwear
fleece/wool garments
shorts
T-shirt

rain gear
hat
gloves
bandanna

Kitchen gear

water purification
stove
windscreen
fuel

lighter/waterproof matches
pot with lid
cup

spoon
pot gripper
biodegradable soap and sponge
food/spices

Toiletries

toothbrush
toothpaste (tiny tube)
comb
biodegradable soap
pack towel

sunscreen
lip balm with sun protection
tampons, pads, or other device to
    catch menstrual flow

moist wipes
extra Ziploc bags and cloth bag
toilet paper (partial roll)

First aid kit

Band-Aids
Neosporin or another antibiotic
    ointment
sterile gauze pads
adhesive tape or duct tape

10cc irrigation syringe with an 18-
    gauge catheter tip for flushing
    out cuts
latex surgical gloves
moleskin or your choice of blister
    coverings

nonaspirin pain reliever
elastic bandage to wrap a hurt
    ankle, knee, elbow, or wrist
needle for splinters or blisters
matches to sterilize needle
first aid book

Depending on where you are traveling, you may also need . . .

compass
pepper spray
rope or parachute cord to hang
    food from bears
spare batteries
sunglasses

sun hat
trekking poles
cards/game
paper/pencil
paperback book
bug repellent

small lantern or candle
repair kit (contents listed below)
watch
camera
trowel

Repair kit

ripstop nylon tape or duct tape
needle, heavy-duty thread, and a
    patch

safety pins
small pocket knife
parachute cord